MW01632943

FROM POVERTY AND ANGER TO PEACE AND CONTENTMENT

CARSON D. LAUFFER

The Healing of a Soul: From Poverty and Anger to Peace and Contentment
Published by Soul Health
Walled Lake, Michigan

ISBN: 978-0-578-81644-9
RELIGION / Comparative Religion

Cover and Interior design by Victoria Wolf,
wolfdesignandmarketing.com

To my blessed wife of over 53 years without whom I could never have completed or even begun this book. God bless you.

To my sons, Christian and Andrew, and their families that they may know the healing of their souls as they follow Christ.

PREFACE

St. Paul, or a close follower, wrote, "For our struggle is not with flesh and blood but with principalities, with the powers, with the rulers of this present darkness, with the evil spirits in the heavens."[1] The author instructs us to put on the whole armor of God. What all of that means is the intent of this writing. It is also to show that in most cultures, this same struggle, this same need, to save or heal our souls is at least a major focus of their thought.

What does it mean when someone says, "We hope this fellow can work out his demons?" Is it just a flippant comment without meaning? Or do we wonder what spirit prompted a fellow to act this way? What happens when one of the most rational nations on earth like Germany foments war and kills many of its own citizens? Was Dr. M. Scott Peck correct when he became convinced that demon possession is a reality and the spirits that drive people to certain actions are something other than simple mental illness?[2]

Many have characterized this period in Western Civilization

as "postmodernist."[3] Or even Solipsistic.[4] It may well be the extreme development of Occam's observation that "plurality should not be posited without necessity."[5] Everything else is speculation. But to understand our present philosophical confusion, we must understand our present age in much more bleak terms. We seem to have reduced all knowledge, from observable reality to immediate reaction, to immediate emotion without reference to either objective reality and without any internal reflection as to its meaning. In other words, we seem to have discounted consciousness entirely and have sold our souls on the altar of artificial intelligence (AI). AI lacks any reflection at all. By succumbing to AI we are becoming only reactors and something less than human. It's enough to make Occam blush.

Has it become impossible for modern man to be conscious of a soul and think beyond reacting to momentary emotion? Are we doomed to self-destruct as a species? Or is there hope that we will find our soul and hence find real peace, true healing, and true salvation not only for each individual but also for the world?

Religion is one of, if not the main pillars of culture. The danger of "demonizing" (there's that word again) religion as is popular today is that we are destroying the foundation of culture itself. We will examine the teachings concerning the soul in some of the most influential religions of the world. We will look not only at the various forms the issue takes in various expressions of Christianity, but we will look at the teachings of Sanatana Dharma and Buddhism.

For this book, I will use my life as a model for the healing of one's soul.

Healing and saving have the same root word. They mean rescue, cleansing, or healing. The soul is the driving principle that activates and coalesces our sense of the divine and the human. This healing is eventually permanent since the soul is on a path of becoming part of being. In the broadest sense, we have viewed this healing in either a limited or universal sense, which leads us to another issue that needs reflection.

The argument between those who believe in universal salvation, on the one hand, and those who believe in limited salvation, has been found in writings since the beginning of writing. I have argued on both sides of the issue. Do souls only reside in the area of becoming or do they return to God and rejoin Being? On the other hand, is each soul created for each body, and their existence is forever bliss or torment? Does the soul precede the individual body or does it not?

Is the soul healed over several physical lifetimes? Or is it healed in one lifetime, which determines its destiny? Are the seers of Sanatana Dharma right when they insist that a soul returns eventually to its creator after karma has been dissipated?

The teaching that has influenced me the most is called in Eastern Christian tradition, *Theosis*. *Theosis* is defined as deification or divinization that is the step-by-step healing of the soul, which results in unification with God. This is best described in this frequently used phrase in the early Church and by many in the Church today, "God became man that we might become God."

I will apply my own personal insights as illustrated from my life through a practical examination of Erik Erikson's eight stages of psychosocial development as expressed in his now-famous study *Childhood and Society*.

For reference, Erikson's eight stages are: Stage 1 Basic Trust vs. Basic Distrust; Stage 2 Autonomy vs. Shame and Doubt; Stage 3 Initiative vs. Guilt; Stage 4 Industry vs. Inferiority; Stage 5 Identity vs. Role Confusion; Stage 6 Intimacy vs. Isolation; Stage 7 Industry vs. Stagnation; Stage 8 Ego Integrity vs. Despair.

Chapter 1

THE SOUL AND ITS HEALING

"Death Came through sin."

—Romans 5:12

"The last enemy to be destroyed is death"

—I Corinthians 15:26

There are two issues with which we must grapple to begin our discussion. First, does the soul exist, and what is the soul? Second, how do we know the soul needs healing, and how is one healed? Once the soul's existence is established, the necessity for its healing will follow.

This study is intended as a discussion starter for the widest possible audience, but we must clear up a few philosophical and theological issues to start.

First, is the soul a necessary entity? Forensic discipline helps in establishing the answer to this question. The first step in developing forensic evidence is to show that something *is*. This is the question of conjecture or in Latin of *on sit*.[6] What evidence exists that the thing we suspect really is or even really exists? Is there such a thing as a soul? Or is the very talk of such an entity sheer folly? Is this an empty, useless discussion that the development of artificial intelligence (AI) makes redundant? Can we program some man-made machine in the future that will make this entire question nonsensical? Will we discover that humans have no such thing as freedom of thought or creation of or the discovery of anything that isn't already programmed into us? Is there a self or is that an illusion? Are we only machines that accidentally came into existence? Or worse, are we all only illusions of each other, or do we exist with some sense of free will that isn't just a pretense? Are our thoughts real, or is the sophistic "philosophy" of solipsism actually all there is?[7] Or are we actually conscious of things that really do exist? If that is true, which seems to follow, then it must be true that some repository for consciousness exists? That repository we call the soul.

A problem exists with our over reliance upon Artificial Intelligence. Google searches are dependent upon them. AI is limited to simply repeating what it has been given. It cannot produce anything new but can only repeat what we already know or believe in a much more rapid way than can human intelligence. Some believe that AI will someday develop a superior intelligence to human intelligence. That is simply and quite frankly impossible. AI is limited from new insight or consciousness of what has not yet been seen. Humans are defined by their consciousness of what has not yet been at least not in any physical sense.

Gilder observes, "Real science shows that the universe is a singularity and thus a creation. Creation is an entropic product of a higher consciousness echoed by human consciousness."[8]

Consciousness is a function of what is almost universally called the soul.

In short, it is impossible for any machine to be designed that can encompass every piece of reality or creativity. Such requires consciousness to approach such abilities. The real world is thus the world of the soul or even greater the infinite. Only the self or the soul can ever have consciousness.

It is clear that the soul is a necessary reality unless one succumbs to the solipsism that nothing is real. Of course, if that were true, even this book and my life and yours aren't real either. Not being interested in absurdities, I'll remain in the realm of reality.

This takes us to the second question that needs to be addressed "what is that which is to be addressed?" It is not enough to declare that something must be. Some effort must be put into discerning what that entity is.

In Greek, the soul is *psyche,* which usually refers to the psychological existence of a person. In Latin, it is *anima*, sometimes understood as soul and sometimes the human spirit. In Sanatana Dharma (Hinduism), it is the true Self.[9] Buddhist teaching denies that this is true but suggests that there is no real soul but only momentary and insubstantial flashes of impressions. This is explained by the doctrine of *anatta*, meaning there is no substantial soul. One of the best explanations of this is found in the teaching of Dependent or Conditional Origination.[10] Existence only happens in those instances when time and space intersect. The next instant when anything happens in space or time that which one might call soul ceases to exist. This is an intriguing idea, but it is unsatisfactory because the doctrine itself is an expression of the *consciousness* of a reality that is not supposed to exist. More could be said, but perhaps a distraction for our discussion. It has caused scholars to reflect upon it for millennia without reaching any consensus on its meaning. Hence, we will not further address *anatta*.[11]

What is left is to describe the qualities of the soul, which will be the essence of the remainder of this book. We will discuss when the soul becomes apparent. What functions the soul serves. How the soul becomes damaged or diseased. And, how the soul may be saved or healed.

The soul enables us to conceive of things that do not yet exist. It connects the physical life to the spiritual. When functioning properly, consciousness and conscience, functions of the soul, can guide us both in the avoidance of evil and in the grasping of a future potential for good.

We know that the soul, our true selves, needs to be saved or healed not only from traditions that come through every culture and from many historical and archaeological records. From wars to human sacrifice, we realize that something is wrong or sick about the soul. We also realize from the vision of and accomplishment of wonderful ideas and accomplishments that the sickness of the soul is not natural to it.

Bhakti Yoga of the great teachings of Sanatana Dharma is filled with stories of the gods and goddesses who attempt to show us ways out of our distress.

Buddhist teachings remind us that the most common element of humanity is *Dukkha* or suffering. The entire teaching is designed to overcome suffering. In fact, the Four Noble Truths, central to all Buddhist teaching, describe the existence, recognition, and the Eightfold path for overcoming suffering.

The idea of the soul is taken for granted in most, if not all, philosophical systems. Presocratic Greek thought saw the soul as the source of animation for the body based upon commonsense notions of reality. Plato understood the soul acting on three levels from the lower function as appetites or eros, spirit or will, and the rational or *logos*. Aristotle conceived the soul as the first actuality or potentiality which toward its fulfillment. Epicurius understood it as the source of commonsense that animates the body of living things. The Stoics had a similar notion, which was used frequently, e.g., Marcus Aurelius *Meditations* refers to the soul as that element which collects perceptions of right and wrong which motivates the body to action.[12] The Neoplatonists saw the soul contemplates and know Divine ideas. A soul's knowledge is inevitably limited, except having returned to the absolute Unity.[13]

Most of these systems had a profound effect upon Christian thought, and they continue up until the present. This is especially true of Neoplatonism and Stoicism, especially as applied to conscience of right and wrong and of the notion of the soul's incompleteness until united with God. One can see these ideas reoccurring in the notion of our return to unity with God, the idea of the purification of the soul through sanctification, and the healing of the soul as in the Greek Theosis.

The Judeo-Christian tradition recalls the fall of humankind through the drive to become God by knowing right from wrong without God. The result drove us away from our true selves, our God created souls. We learn how children understand intuitively the presence of God and of our true selves, but tend to lose that understanding as we age. A certain persistence is necessary in order to keep that knowledge. If we do not persist through learning with both the rational mind and with our heart, we can lose track of ourselves. Common expressions reflect not only the loss of that identity but the imposition of spiritual forces that influence or even possess us. What does it mean to say that someone has been influenced by demons? What does it mean that someone has overcome his demons? What are the principalities and powers that are not seen but are present which St. Paul describes thusly, "For our struggle is not with flesh and blood, but with the principalities and powers, with the world rulers of this present darkness, with the evil spirits in the heavens?" (Ephesians: 6:12).

Let's get started.

Chapter 2

AUTONOMY OR SHAME

"Blessed be the God and Father of our Lord Jesus Christ who has blessed us in Christ with every spiritual blessing in the heavens, as He chose us in Him, before the foundation of the world, to be holy and without blemish before Him. In love, He destined us for adoption to Himself through our Lord Jesus Christ, in accord with the favor of His will, for the praise of the glory of His grace that he granted us in the beloved"

—(Ephesians 1:3-6).[14]

This examines Erikson's Stage 2 of a person's psychosocial development in his groundbreaking study on the stages of psychosocial development, *Childhood and Society*.

Stage 1 is infancy, "Trust vs. Mistrust." I will mostly by-pass this stage since it is totally pre-memory. It has to do with whether the infant learns to let his mother out of sight without undue anxiety or rage. I have seen some children who suffered from severe neglect and never learned to trust anyone or anything. I apparently survived this stage. To put it within the context of the development of the soul seems to go something like this: The animating element of life is the soul. He/she must learn to trust and respond to trustworthy activities. Breastfeeding, as my mother kindly did, developed a sense of trust in my nascent soul. No development can take place without this. Mother's and, to a lesser degree, father's, begins the journey back to the soul's maker.

Stage 2 explores "Autonomy vs. Shame and Doubt." This is an examination of how a healthy individual gains a sense of autonomy by overcoming shame and doubt.

This is the stage in which the child must learn to stand on his own feet.[15] While doing so, the child must learn to do so without experiencing the sense of being watched "with pants down."[16] The child learns "self-control without losing self-esteem."[17] This is the stage in which the soul can move on its own toward a true standing.

"How is it," my friend Alice asked, "that you have been chosen to do and to be who you are? God has put his hand on your shoulder to accomplish what you accomplish."

It's one thing to believe this academically. I had been taught this and had taught this most of my life. But to understand that it is recognized by someone else caught me by surprise and forced some serious reflection. I felt like I was just some dumb kid born to a struggling, rather poor family. In their way, they were making some effort to survive and had some basic understanding of honesty, but they really cared very little for creating a better life for themselves. Or, more charitably, they may not have known how or were incapable of developing a better life. Like many people in our small village of Jasper in Southeast Michigan, they argued over things that really didn't matter. They were insecure to the point that any little thing could set them off in another round of endless blaming.

They were profane and loud. "Go to hell." "G-d damn you." "I wish you were dead." "I wish you were never born" were common expressions heard not only at every meal, but every time they got within each other's view. As I matured, I could not understand why they got married or how they managed to produce six children.

When my mother stayed home to focus on raising a family, my father would criticize her for never contributing to the finances. When she was able to get a job as a practical nurse at the nursing home and bought something for the house, my father would criticize her choice as a waste of money. When my father would try hard to make some money for the family, my mother would criticize him for not making enough to get us out of poverty. Privately, my mother often recounted how my father tried to get her to abort me before I was born. When I was young, I did not understand why she told me that and, frankly, still don't see the purpose in it. Nor did I understand why my father took his frustrations out on my mother or out on his children.

There were better moments, less destructive, but the struggle and apparent hatred for each other was always there. Still, here I was, the only person in our family and as far as I ever knew, in our extended family of aunts and uncles and cousins to not only ever complete college but several years of graduate education and had served not only on a faculty of a small college but also was still pastoring churches.

When my old friend said that God had placed his hand on my shoulder, I began thinking of times when that seemed absolutely true. My struggle for autonomy was successful.

When I was five, my mother called to me and asked me for help. She was in terrific pain, and I was her first-born child. By that time, in the early 1950s, I already had a little sister and a toddler brother. My father was out for the evening. He was an owner and dealer and repairman in a very small business in a tiny town and was often gone for the evening. Sometimes he delivered appliances or tires or something from his little shop. Sometimes he was elsewhere. I did not know where.

My mother begged me to phone for help. She needed a doctor, or she needed my dad.

Those were the days before we had a dial phone. I'm not sure if I had ever even used our candle phone before. My grandparents had a dial phone, but they lived in the big city many miles north of us. They might as well have been on the other side of the world as far as my efforts to get to them. I did not know how to call them. I had no transportation to get the seven miles to reach them, and I doubt that at five, I could even have found them. My mom needed help immediately, and I was the point man for getting it.

I knew that if I cranked the handle on the side of the box hanging on the wall, it would alert some lady on the other end, and I might even hear some other people talking on the party line. I climbed up on the chair near the table on which the phone sat. I cranked the handle on the box on the wall as I put the receiver to my ear. Thankfully, no one else was talking on the phone, so I was able to speak to the lady on the other end of the phone wire. I explained the predicament I was in and that I did not know how to make phone calls. She assured me that she could help me find my dad, but I had no idea where he was.

I mentioned a few names, but he wasn't there. I had heard that sometimes he frequented what the people called the beer garden. The local one was owned by a bald-headed man named Schaeffer. He and his wife were known for having horrendous fights, even leading to Schaeffer shooting a gun at his wife. The bullet missed. His attempt failed, as was rumored, because of Schaeffer's drunken stupor. The nice lady called there, but he wasn't there.

The next town with a beer garden was a few miles away. She found him there. What seemed like hours but was less than half an hour before my father arrived home. My mother was trying to avoid pregnancy for a fourth child, but the IUD had punctured my mother's uterus. Apparently, it did not cause permanent damage. A few months later, she was pregnant once again.

During that pregnancy, I began to detect the pathway to saving a soul, but I did not yet realize it. Helping my mother was a hint, but something happened with my mother's pregnancy that lit a light.

Had God included me in His plan from before the foundation of the world? Had my soul been deemed precious in God's opinion, so much so that I did not have to live as I was taught to live? Was this because He had created my soul from before the foundation of the world? Or was that because He knew He would create my soul long before He actually created it? Was His plan to save me for the salvation of others? Or was I picked out when others were not?

In what way was I to be made or was being made 'holy and blameless"? Was the salvation of my soul just for me and would be accomplished just by God and me?

At five, I did not know how to answer these questions, let alone how to form them, but they were there because they developed even as I saw how my mother survived a brutal attack and as I helped save some puppies.

Chapter 3

GUILT OR INITIATIVE

"Give me a life wherever there is an opportunity to live, and better life than was my father's."

—Sophocles, *Oedipus Rex*

Stage 3 describes Initiative vs. Guilt. Guilt is described as the castration complex. Initiative is the joyful sense of accomplishing something on one's own. If the child is held back from initiative, he carries guilt. Yet, "a child is at no time more ready to learn quickly and avidly, to become bigger in the sense of sharing obligation and performance than during this period of his development."[18]

Guilt is both a gift and a barrier. It is a gift of growth and direction in the soul to guide it toward holiness by blocking its way from moral turpitude. At the same time, the guilt is a movement toward initiating right activities.[19]

My mother recovered from that trauma, but a new one was on the horizon.

Before we reflect upon the events as I approached my sixth year, it is important to understand the events around the choosing of my senior pictures, especially by my mother. In those days, I wore what was then called a flat top. The style was still popular in the 1960s and took little care. Since my father did the haircutting for the boys in the family, it was easier to cut as well. I did get a special flat top from the local barber in preparation for my pictures. What I liked most was that it made me believe I looked like a popular wrestler of those days, Dick the Bruiser. Another advantage of the haircut was that I could look either happy or severe without much effort.

The photographer took some pictures that made me look happy, and some that made me look severe. I assumed that my parents would choose the happy look. My father didn't care, but my mother made a choice that surprised me at the time. She chose without hesitation the severe pose. Later events made the reason for that choice quite clear, and as I reflect upon the events that took place just as I was turning six, quite obvious.

It began long before my birth. During the Great Depression, my father was a sharecropper who, through hard work, had been able to buy an Oliver tractor and some equipment with what was called a chattel mortgage. He worked the land the best he could, only to find himself unable to make enough money to keep up the payments on his equipment. The County Sheriff conducted a sale that never left my father's memory nor his way of looking at his own life. I never saw my father weep. But as a twenty-something-year-old man trying to make a go of it during the Depression, and seeing everything go at pennies on a dollar, he cried. He never got over the humiliation. He was a failure in his own eyes, and nothing he did, not his marriages, his later businesses, or his six children, could heal his soul from that devastation. He was married for ten years, but his first wife was unfaithful, and it ended in divorce. His second wife, our mother, was twelve and a half years younger than he was.

She, too, was affected by her earlier life.

My mother's mother was the disciplinarian in their household. When my grandmother disciplined my mother, it was to her father that she turned. She often went to him, and he would say, "Would you like Daddy to take you for some turtle soup?" This seemed strange to me, but as she explained, "Daddy would take me to a local restaurant that specialized in turtle soup. That represented our special time together. We would walk downtown to the restaurant together and talk until I calmed down." She loved her daddy but resented her mother. She married an older man to fill in for her daddy.

Then the event took place that presented the problem that moved me toward the struggle between initiative and guilt or Stage 3 in Erikson's study of psychosocial development.

One day shortly after my sixth birthday, my dad's anger over what he perceived as a failed life and my mother's confusion over her choice of a marriage partner boiled over in a terrible way.

During a meal, which one doesn't matter, because the scene was always the same, they got into another of their endless arguments. My mother was eight months pregnant at this time. My dad was frustrated that he could barely support the three children they already had. Something happened that had never happened before. This time my mother landed on her back on the floor, and my father was over her pounding her body and face.

I yelled at him, but he would not listen. I wanted to attack him, but I froze. What was I supposed to do? I was as emotionally bankrupt at that moment as my father had been when he went bankrupt so many years earlier. I was completely helpless in that situation. I was guilty as hell, and I was lost.

I knew I was lost. Who was I? What was I doing? I understood that I was conscious of myself, and I did not like who or what I was. To be self-conscious is to be aware that one is primarily a soul, but my soul was lost. The soul is the activating principle of life, determined by some sense of initiative. I could do nothing and was even afraid to try. The soul initiates, but I could not initiate anything that I knew was right. Aggressively opposing or overcoming my father in order to save my mother was something I was incapable of doing.

The impulse to save women attacked by men came to be a recurring theme in my life. Thankfully, I was often more successful later in life. But I knew I did not wish to behave toward others as my father behaved toward my mother.

My little brother, Willie, was born a month later. For all of his life, he suffered from asthma. I wondered for years if my father's beating had caused his problem.

I sensed I had something in me that wanted to do something to save my mother, but I was not able to do a thing. There was a redemption of sorts a few months later, but it was becoming clear to me that my life was not just a series of unrelated events. I was not a machine. I was a living soul developing my conscience and my consciousness of myself, others, and of another presence.

Chapter 4

THE INDUSTRIAL AGE: INDUSTRY VS. INFERIORITY

"Sloth makes all things difficult, but industry all things easy."

—Benjamin Franklin

Stage 4 examines Industry vs. Inferiority. Erikson states that from the ages of six to eleven, children learn to be industrious, or they learn inferiority through failure. This very often occurs as children enter grammar school and learn to accomplish things through industrious effort, or they learn to fail. It's an essential stage in the healing and growth of the soul.[20] For me, this happened dramatically when I was about seven. It was a life-changing experience and one that has served me well throughout my life.

Sometime in my fourth or fifth year, my parents bought a

purebred female boxer pup. Since she was golden in color, they gave her an obvious name, Golden Lady. When they tried to register that name so they could breed her, they discovered that Golden Lady was already in use. They made an official change in her name, but we knew her always as Goldie.

By the time she was two or three, and I was about seven, my parents decided to breed Goldie. Before dawn, there was a great commotion both inside and outside of the house. It appeared my father was very busy with something early in the morning, but at first, we did not know what. As we quickly learned, Goldie was delivering her pups.

Goldie delivered her one and only litter of pups. The delivery almost killed her. Perhaps she was too young. I never knew. But she was neutered after the experience. Out of the five pups that survived the birth, only three were healthy. The smallest were runts who could not feed themselves and were not expected to live even through the day, and certainly not through the next night.

I think because I was the eldest child, my parents were willing to allow me more responsibility than the others. There was another influence, which I was beginning to sense in my mind. This influence was something or someone both outside and inside of me.

I knew somehow that I should take action. I asked my parents if I could try to feed these pups. After they agreed to let me try to, and after they warned me that it might not work, we found an eyedropper. We warmed some milk, prepared a bed for the pups, and I set about to feed and watch them for as long as it took.

The family went to bed, and I sat down for my vigil. All throughout the night, I watched the pups and fed them with warm milk when they seemed willing to receive it. By morning the pups were moving about and even opened their eyes. Soon they all were feeding at their mother's breast.

My sense of inferiority over my inability to protect my mother soon dissipated and was replaced by a sense of usefulness. There were things I could do on my own. I was able to follow the lead of the other reality to save some puppies, no matter how long it took.

Would my life lead to the saving of others? I wasn't sure, but it certainly seemed so in that moment.

Over the next several years, as I discovered my identity, I thought back on that evening and night and began to understand my identity.

Chapter 5

THE PREACHER AND ST. COMFORT

"If you want to know what your purpose in life is, come to the altar and give your life to Christ."

—Preacher, July 1960, at the Holiness Camp meeting near Deerfield, Michigan

The fifth stage of Erikson's description of psychosocial development describes the struggle between identity and confusion.[21] The prime directive in my life came into focus.

It wasn't that my parents never sent me to Sunday School at the Evangelical United Brethren Church, but that they never went. I did enjoy the hour or so away from the house, but I was not fully conscious of the God of the Church.

By 1960, my parents, Paul and Ruth, had six children. The three oldest were in elementary or Junior High School. On Sundays, my father had established a Sunday tradition of going fishing with his buddy Earl. That left my mother home alone with six children, all under thirteen. I think she sent us off to Sunday School so she could get a little time alone.

I was beginning to realize that though my mother loved us in her own way, the pressure of six children, an unappreciative and sometimes violent husband, and sheer loneliness were causing her to have bouts of severe depression. She had just the medicine for it. Didn't the Bible itself recommend "wine for the stomach's sake?"

Well, it wasn't wine. That was well above our financial station, but beer could be purchased for twenty cents a bottle or can and could be purchased for thirty-five cents at Schaffer's.

My mother had found this medicine to her liking some years before she and my father met. She was arrested for under-age drinking and, as my father put it many times during their frequent yelling matches, was on "prohibition" when they met. I believe he met probation, but I never asked him.

My mother often recounted a story that puzzled me. Why would she confess to an offense that my father frequently accused her of, and why would she confess it to her prepubescent son?

As my mother often recounted the event, one night at the age of nineteen my mother came home drunk to her parents' home. My mother stood about five foot eight, but her mother was only about five foot one. However, my grandma was one tough woman. She blocked the door and told her that she was not welcome to enter. My mother insisted that she was going to enter the house and raised her hand to shove or maybe hit her mother. Before she could accomplish her task, my grandmother knocked her to the floor of the porch.

My mother had a drinking problem that pre-dated her marriage by at least three years by my mother's own confession. My father's behavior was not one I wished to emulate, at least in his treatment of my mother nor in the disciplinary treatment of his children. But he had a reason to dislike my mother's behavior. My mother was not innocent, but neither one tried very hard to understand the other.

I've mentioned my father's mistreatment of my mother and my mother's passive-aggressive treatment toward him. I've also mentioned the strange interchange with me, as if she longed for me to be the kind, tolerant father of her childhood years. But my father was the disciplinarian in our family. His approach was never to discuss with us our misbehavior or to try to find out why we did what we did. His approach was forceful and sometimes even brutal.

Children have accidents from time to time. My sister, who was fifteen months younger than I, often wet the bed. This was more or less tolerated until she was about six or seven, but after that, she received corporal punishment in the mornings after she wet the bed. She received it from my father, who would force her to remove her panties, and he would strap her with his belt.

She, however, got off easy compared with her younger brother. Jimmy wet the bed almost every night. For every night he did, my father whipped him on the bare bottom also before he was sent to school.

My mother could not stop him. I could not stop him. From my eighth year and into Junior High School, this was the morning routine at our house. I desperately wanted to run away. But a countervailing reality also pulled at me. I was conscious of better realities because I had heard reports of them. I somehow knew that not all families lived like this, but I had no first-hand knowledge of them. Still, that knowledge was informing me and making me, the soul or self that is me, into a person that knew there had to be a better way to live, and I was determined to find it.

I had begun to hitchhike to Adrian on Sundays to attend a small holiness church with my grandparents. It was six miles away. I couldn't do it every Sunday. Sometimes my father would go fishing, and other times, my mother would just be gone, leaving me to watch my younger siblings for the day.

My grandparents invited me to go to a Holiness Camp Meeting just outside of Deerfield, Michigan. I wasn't sure what to expect. I had never gone to one before and only ever heard of one from the preacher at the Holiness Church or from my grandparents themselves.

It was a hot summer evening in July 1960. My grandfather drove the Plymouth down a country path, which was hardly a road, until we reached a clearing at what seemed to be a rather large wooden structure, which they called the tabernacle. I noticed that the sides of the building were propped open for air circulation. It was greatly needed. Eventually, nearly 200 people filled the building.

The music was lively and appealing to me. It was an exciting atmosphere. People really got into the singing. One fellow got so excited that he ran from the back of the room to the front on top of the backs of the pews. He then jumped aboard what was called the Altar or Mourners Bench alternately and ran across it. He then jumped atop the pews and ran all the way to the back. All the time, he shouted praises to God. I could barely imagine such a place. People were shouting and running about, but they were not angry. No one attacked anyone, and they used the various names for God in very praiseworthy ways. What a change from the daily routines where I grew up.

The preacher, whom they called the evangelist, had a forceful but to me very appealing sermon, which didn't seem to last very long but was probably an hour or so. Then he gave the invitation that appealed to me more than any I had ever heard.

"If you want to know what your purpose in life is, come to the altar and give your life to Christ." He did not have to say it twice. The people were singing these lyrics:

Softly and tenderly Jesus is calling,
Calling for you and for me;
See, on the portals He's waiting and watching,
Watching for you and for me.

Refrain:
Come home, come home,
You who are weary, come home;
Earnestly, tenderly, Jesus is calling,
Calling, O sinner, come home!

I don't recall hearing any of the verses after that. My soul, as poorly formed as it was up to that point, was yearning to find a purpose in life. But mostly, I was yearning to find a way of life that was not filled with the hatred that my parents expressed. I had no desire to grow up and treat others as my parents treated each other, and as we were treated. I didn't need to be asked more than once to come home since where I was living was not any kind of home that I desired, and since Jesus, this cosmic figure, was dealing out the invitation, I went happily to the altar and said, "Here I am. Here's my soul. Make me whatever you wish."

Later in life, I studied John Bunyan's *Pilgrim's Progress* and recognized myself in it. Even later I studied St. John Climacus', *The Ladder of Divine Ascent* with which I fully identified. Both describe the journey of a soul upward toward the awaiting Jesus Christ.

It was not surprising that I took this step just as I was reaching puberty. Most serious early conversions take place during this period in a person's life. The confusion was over. My soul was identified as belonging to Jesus Christ. It was also identified in a very specific way. Given my later growth, it is no surprise that this was a holiness camp meeting. The expectation from the beginning was that I would develop. That this was simply the beginning. I expected that any conversions in the future would be based upon this primary conversion but would be an advance upon this. And so, it was to be.

At age fifteen, I was able to go to this denomination's Youth Bible Camp in Circleville, Ohio. Since this was sanctioned by my grandparents, I was eager to go. There was great singing and preaching with many seminars and many great outdoor activities. I remember enjoying the week immensely.

On Monday, the announcement was made that all "preacher boys" would have a chance to give a four-minute sermon on

Thursday. I began thinking that perhaps this was my calling. The fact that I jumped into the chance of saving my mom and our puppies was that of the Holy Spirit? I only later learned that the movement of God was described in many ways in most religions. Moreover, I wondered if my wish to try to protect my mom from my dad was the start of my true identity. I often wondered if, somehow, this drawing began well before I was born.

I immediately went to my bunk side and knelt with my Bible. The only way I knew to find important answers was through a youth activity I enjoyed. It was called a Bible Drill or a Sword Drill alternately, as in sword of the Lord, drill. So naively, or was it providentially, I put the Bible above my head. Then I closed my eyes, put the Bible on the bunk, and opened the book. Then I placed my finger on this passage: "Seek first the Kingdom of God and His righteousness and all these things shall be added unto you. Take therefore no thought for the morrow: for the morrow shall take thought for the things of itself. Sufficient unto the day is the evil thereof." That was from the King James Version of the Bible, Matthew 6:33–34. At that point in my life, what other version could it be?

It struck me like thunder. To me, this was a confirmation of what I was to do with my life and for the rest of my life. It was also the text I was to use for the short sermon I was to preach later that week.

The sermon itself was not so good. For one thing, I had underlined the words so much that I could barely read them. Nevertheless, I never felt so confident that this was my identity than I did during those four minutes.

Then came the man I call St. Comfort. I never called him that in his presence, but from when I was sixteen to eighteen years old, no person on earth was more of a comfort to me as the ironically named Comfort Stephens.

Comfort was and had been for many years a traveling ambassador for a soul on his way to heaven and was by his winsomeness pulling people in his wake. He was seventy-six when I met him, and he walked through the streets of Adrian smiling and whistling almost constantly. It's not always safe to trust people who smile all of the time, but Comfort was a rare exception. People who didn't know him well would stop him and ask, "why are you so happy." He would tell them without hesitation, "I love Jesus and am on my way to meet Him" or something similar. He would visit various holiness churches in the city and in the nearby area. By this time, I was alternating between my Grandparents Church of Christ in Christian Union and the area Church of the Nazarene. It was at the latter location that I met him. His joyful countenance attracted me to him.

It wasn't long before he was inviting me to come by his house any Sunday that I was in town.

We spoke of holiness and how we might live it. He showed me scriptures and helped me understand their meaning in ways I never understood before. Most of all, here was an old man full of life who treated me as an actual human being. Most people did not do that. I would never leave his presence without us praying together. I grew more and more in my love for Jesus and my love for His people. Occasionally we would travel to one church or another or to a camp meeting.

His life had not been easy. He told me of losing a daughter and then of losing his wife. But everything he encountered in life seemed to make him more and more like my vision of Jesus. My travels with St. Comfort only covered two years during my Junior and Senior years of high school but they were glorious. I went off to college and shortly learned of his death. After his death, I began to find it natural to pray to him. We were fellow travelers, and from his example, I learned why despite the fact that our souls must develop in the way they will and in that path, there is loneliness, but we are, in fact, never alone.

This part of learning about myself, about the soul and its healing, is difficult to learn until we understand that the function of conscience is a part of the soul. I'll discuss more about conscience and its cluster of meanings in a later chapter. But for now, "common sense" is a somewhat adequate way of looking at it. Syneidesis (Gr) or Conscientia (Ln) means to know together. This knowledge is the basis of natural law and is one aspect of the soul that grows and heals. The content of the knowledge is something like universals common to all humans and, in spiritual terms, point us to our connection with God.

These teen years were not simple. I was counted on more and more to babysit my younger siblings as both of my parents were absent most weekends, but they were rarely together.

One Sunday, a couple of guys came around in a pink and grey Nash and asked me if I knew where Ruth was. I had no idea. Why would two guys I never met but obviously knew me, ask if I knew where my mother was and call her by her first name? A few weeks later, I was to find out.

I had watched my brothers and sisters for most of the day, but I was able to arrange for a ride to church that evening. My mother had promised to be home by the afternoon. It was getting late, and she was still not home, so I walked down to Shaeffer's Tavern to try to get her to come home. She was sitting with these two guys I had seen a few weeks earlier and enjoying their company with some beers. I did not get to church that evening.

As winter approached, another such occurrence with these men came to light. Again I walked down toward the tavern as just as I got to the corner where a streetlight was I saw my mother sitting in the front seat between these two men. As they approached the corner and saw me, they made a U-turn and drove away.

About two a.m. one morning, my father woke me up and asked me to go with him to try to track down my mother. After searching for a couple of hours and not finding her, we returned home.

Despite all of this, both of my parents turned to me for help. Why was that so? I don't know for sure. Did they even know why they depended upon me, a teenager, for help?

My parents divorced after I went off to college. She married one of the men she hung out with and remained so for eleven years. That relationship allowed my mother to drink beers from sunrise to sunset. She ate very little and began to sink into dementia. He died, but my mother lived on for a few years. When asked to whom she was married she would always say, Paul Lauffer. When people asked her about her second husband she answered in indignation, "I've only been married once, and that was to Paul Lauffer."

As she neared the end of her life, she didn't recognize any of us.

Then there was the very shapely girl who wore hot pants and a halter top. I was never so tempted in my life to abandon the soul that was being healed. Somehow, an interior voice kept telling me that my life was in God's hands, and He had a greater purpose. Did I avoid the temptation because I was holy? I doubt it. Did I avoid it because of my father's warnings about venereal disease? Whatever it was, desire for holiness or fear of syphilis, it kept me from living a life in hell in this life and perhaps in the next. The very attractive young lady sent me a tear-filled letter, with actual tear spots, about a week later and begged me to stay with her.

Temptation never ends.

St. Comfort was always a help through these trials and temptation. He was and is a great comfort.

Even these temptations were preparing me for my next step in healing, and there I was to meet St. Christine. She was my escort into Stage 6 or intimacy vs. isolation.

Chapter 6

INTIMACY AND ST. CHRISTINE

"A virtuous woman is a crown to her husband"

—Proverbs 12:4

"But if they cannot contain, let them marry: for it is better to marry than to burn."

—I Corinthians 7:9

In this stage, a person seeks to "fuse identity with another and gain ethical strength to abide by the commitment."[22] The entrance into Stage 6 took a few years, but now I moved into Erikson's Stage 6 from Isolation to Intimacy. It occurred in this fashion. It can be a clumsy, even difficult movement, but it is essential to the existence of the soul and its movement toward the holy.

Our school was six miles away from our home. I rode a

school bus until graduation from high school. After my experience of receiving "the Call" as it was called, I began conducting Bible Studies with younger children on our way to school. It seemed natural. Younger children would flock around me to hear my Bible stories. It felt good to try in my own way to guide people toward what I understood to be holiness.

I was still surprised at the gift my parents gave me upon graduation. It was a King James Version of the Bible. King James was the only one people in our area trusted. It was a Bible published by Zondervan Publishing called The Marked Reference Bible "Marked by the best methods of Bible Marking on all subjects connected with the themes of salvation, the Holy Spirit, Temporary blessings, and Prophetic subjects." For anyone, I knew this was the very best Bible any preacher of the Gospel could have. It is still today the most cherished gift my parents ever gave me.

How can it be that such angry people also had such loving hearts?

Both my mother and father inscribed it.

May 25, 1965

"My darling son, this the greatest of books we give you with the proud knowledge that it will always be your guide. Prayerfully yours, Mother."

"Many stumbling block (sic) may be in your path, but can be overcome by faith and courage, for they that are weak fall by

> *the wayside. So keek (sic) up the good faith. For a great son, Carson D. Lauffer, your Father."*

The author's identity is unknown to me, but the saying, "God can heal a broken heart, but He has to have all the pieces," came alive for me. Some of the pieces were coming together. Until that moment, I had not seen my parents in that way. Some years later, I saw my father's tombstone on which was simply written: Father. What was most surprising was that he designed his own tombstone. He was most proud of his role as father. I know I responded to seeing it for the first time with, "I did not know he cared about such things." I still don't know if I said that out loud or said it only to myself.

I worked all summer to save up some money for college. I had been accepted at a Christian College, in part, because it was a Christian college and, in part, because this one was fully accredited. I did not even look to a big-time university because I had no confidence that, given my education in a rural high school, I was prepared for such a university. Besides, I was only able to save $40.00 from my summer's work minus the rent I paid to stay home.

With my $40.00 and my belongings in a cardboard box and a small cardboard suitcase, and a one-way ticket on a Greyhound bus, I was off to Kankakee, Illinois, to Olivet Nazarene College via Chicago. I was eighteen with very little money and only a promise of an interview for a job. But I was free.

I realized how free I was when the bus came up out of Lower Wacker Drive in Chicago and saw the brilliant lights on all of the buildings and felt that I must have died and gone to heaven. I had never seen anything like this. I had never been in a large city before, at least not one as large as Chicago and never at night.

Before my journey to Olivet, I had secured an appointment for an interview for full-time employment at Kankakee State Hospital. If I had not eventually been hired, I had no real source of income for college. I was living on faith. I was very thankful that my hopes were not dashed. I had no desire to go back home.

During my freshman year, I was enrolled in a rather large required course that changed my life forever. It was a fine arts course. Imagine a country hick trying to understand sights and sounds I had never been exposed to before. I had no idea how such a course would prepare me to be a pastor or prepare me for anything else, for that matter. Was I ever in for a glorious surprise!

I had a three-piece suit with a reversible vest that I had purchased to attend the junior-senior prom at high school. That was the only suit I had, but it was the finest clothes I owned. It was the clothing I wore for church and the clothing I would wear to any occasion that called for the best I had.

For the prior two summers, I had saved up money to buy my first new suit. Robert Hall had just what I needed for the grand total of $39.00.

In mid-April 1966, it was announced that the entire group, made up of several fine arts students made up of several classes, would be taking busses to the Art Institute of Chicago. Of course, I wore my three-piece suit. It was inconceivable that anyone would travel to such a prestigious place with everyday clothing.

On May 5, 1966, several busses left for Chicago. Upon boarding the bus, I scanned it to see who I might know and what clothing they were wearing. To my dismay, I noticed that everyone was dressed in my words like ungrateful slobs. Everyone except one very cute young woman who wore a nice green and white empire-waisted dress. Throughout the entire trip, I was hoping against hope to talk with this nice young lady. As it turns out, we spent most of the visit together.

We found ourselves breaking away from the group, and suddenly, we stood in front of El Greco's "Assumption of the Virgin." Its elongated figures expressed a stretching toward heaven. I thought and expressed, "that's an el Greco." I was very confident in my pronouncement, which even surprised me. She never told me whether or not she already knew that. I think she was as much interested in me as I was in her. She expressed an appreciation for my knowledge.

She became my bride thirteen months later.

Ah, intimacy.

We set up house in a 50' x 10' mobile home on campus. For several months our grocery bills were carefully kept under $10.00 per week, which was very frugal even for the 1960s. We had each other.

It was sometimes bumpy because we both had to work, and we were both tired much of the time. But we worked out our disagreements. My grades even began to improve. Chrissy was proofreading my papers, and suddenly, fewer red marks came back with the grades.

On Sundays, we traveled several miles off campus to help

start a mission church. We were tired but fulfilled and looked forward to the wonderful years together.

A few months after our marriage, my brother Jim informed me of a discovery he had made. He found a copy of the Lauffer History published in 1906. I was surprised to learn that a group of Doctors named Lauffer in Pennsylvania had researched and published a history of our family that demonstrated our roots in Western Germany and Eastern France. I was especially drawn to a village named after my parents, Laufferville. The details were fascinating, but what interested me the most was the pedigrees of the authors. Not all of them were doctors but the primary ones were. I knew of no one in our present extended family, who had even gone to college. My grandfather Lauffer had a teaching degree from what was known as a teacher's college. He died when I was five. Outside of him, I had no cousins or aunts or uncles who had even gone to college, and no one on my mother's side of the family, either. I've later learned of a few relatives who have degrees, but at the time, I knew of none.

Socially, I knew I had married up, or should I say, in her graciousness, Christine bent down to lift me up. In either case, we were equals in our desire to serve Christ and His Church, and we were compatible in our desire to learn and do the best we could.

My wife's name is Christine, which, of course, means "follower of Christ." The meaning came to me slowly, but it began to dawn on me when after some bouts of frustration that I had not accomplished much as a student or complained at how hard it was to learn foreign languages, she would say, "think about the long route you've traveled. God has taken you places no one else in your family has ever traveled." Or she would say, "remember where you started."

Then there were the times I was so tired from working full time that I could not edit some of my college papers. She never complained. She would edit them, and my grades would go up. Obviously, Christine had gifts in areas I did not. Yet she loved me so much that what I could not do she made holy. It was her patients with me that helped me do well in college, and I believe her love for me softened my rough edges so that she also did well in college.

My first two years of college, which included Greek, were not filled with superlative grades. However, after marriage, my grades steadily went up. I owe the completion of my education to St. Christine, and for that, I will always be grateful. Her willingness to try new things with me and to encourage me as I struggled to grow has been the greatest blessing of my life.

The one thing I could not make possible was the completion of my dissertation for the PhD at Northwestern University. I had completed my Master of Arts and was well on my way to completing research for a study of the early years of Christianity of the idea of conscience/consciousness in the Late Antique period of the Roman Empire. My focus was on the cluster of ideas surrounding the Latin *Conscientia* in the writings of Tertullian. Tertullian was a legally trained and influential Christian who lived in North Africa. His *De Anima*, On the Soul, was fertile ground for understanding the concept, but he used it in most of his writings. Actually, Tertullian's writings form the basis of much of Western Christianity even into modern times. I compare Tertullian and Origen on the issues of the soul in another chapter.

While St. Christine supported the family during this period, I worked on finishing my project even to the point of doing research alone at the University of Glasgow with the late Professor WHC Frend and at the University of Oxford with the late Professor Stanley Lawrence Greenslade. Those were heady days, but also lonely days. We could not afford for both of us to go, but Chrissy sent me off with her blessings.

One day I was researching some monographs on the subject when I ran into two whose titles looked potentially either hopeful or destructive of my efforts. *Conscientia de Tertuliano* was a careful discussion of every use of the term in the writings of Tertullian as was the German study *Conscientia bei Tertullianon*. As I slowly read through each, it became obvious that, for the most part, they had reached the same conclusions I had.

The choice I made was the most difficult I had had to make in my life. Where could I turn for advice? How could I write a dissertation when others had already done the work? I could probably have written it without reference to these monographs, and no one would have been the wiser, except for me. For that matter, I probably would have reached some different conclusions than these researchers had, but given the thoroughness of the monographs I had little way of knowing.

I know what I should have done, but I had the mask I was trying to uphold of my family's most accomplished member. I did not wish to fail, as my father had believed he did. I did not wish to cheat by writing something that I knew had already been written. Most of all, I did not wish to fail my faithful wife.

For over a year, I tried to find a different approach to the subject. Could I broaden my research beyond Tertullian's writing? Could I find a different way of examining the issue? I failed. I failed myself. I failed my beloved wife. There were many tears shed and for an inordinate amount of time. Later, my wife told me that she seriously considered leaving me during that time, and frankly, I would not have blamed her.

My father told me a story that I have recalled several times since. In the early 1950s Western Electric, which sold many of the things my father sold as an independent dealer, offered him a franchise and guaranteed him $13,000 per year. He turned down the offer because he was concerned that he might be forced to do some things that he did not wish to do or to sell materials he did not consider to be good materials. Over the years, that decision wore on him, and as the family grew, he felt guilty or at least conflicted over his decision. He never found a way out of his conflict.

I never found another way to write the work. I never cheated either, for all the good it did. I knew that was not the way out either. For better or worse, that became a block to the healing of my soul for forty-five years. There have been very few days since then that I did not feel guilt for that misstep. St. Christine and I have done many wonderful things since then. I know that it does no good to beat oneself up over the past. But I have, until God has begun rescuing me now through this book, and through the continued loyalty and love of my wife, St. Christine, I may be finding healing.

The Intimacy that God has given me through Christine has really made me blossom. I frequently apologized for allowing guilt to paralyze me. We have wept together over this failure. I've had many dreams over what might have been and many others that caused me to wake up in a sweat. She could have left me, and I would not have blamed her, but when I could not make things real, she made them holy by her loyalty and love.

A brief recounting of some of those things is important to show the beauty and the gifts of one who has been the major part of my healing. She has remained at my side even with the thorn in my flesh, if the soul is of flesh or corporeal, in the view of Tertullian.

I was an Ordained Deacon in the United Methodist Church. This could be a permanent order or a transitional order onto the order of Elders. I had not decided. I asked the bishop for an assignment in a Church. It would allow me the opportunity to work for another year on my dissertation for the PhD, and if I could not complete it, I would enter the Master of Divinity program at Garrett-Evangelical Seminary in preparation for Ordination as an Elder. After a year of very good success in the parish and no real progress on the dissertation, I gave that up and decided to enter seminary to complete my Master of Divinity degree.

The event was potentially catastrophic. We were driving south on Harlem Avenue in Worth, Illinois, heading back toward the church when I finally told my beloved Christine that I was giving up my effort for the PhD. After all her sacrifice and our mutual hope, she was devastated. But she did not leave me. This turning point occurred in the summer of 1979.

I decided then to complete my Master of Divinity degree

and to enter the United Methodist Ministry. I described it as climbing a tree, and when the topmost branch broke off, I caught myself on the next lower one. Self-pity is never accurate and never attractive. But there it was.

In the midst of my self-pity, my beloved St. Christine found a Government Document, *The Dictionary of Occupational Titles*, which evaluated five categories of intelligence and what level of each was required for each vocation. It measured various kinds of political, legal, and creative careers. There were thousands of careers evaluated. Each level was measured on a five-point scale. We examined different vocations. My beloved was beguiling me into a life's lesson in a very gentle and beneficial way. She pointed out Clergy, and we looked at the level of intelligence required for each category of intellectual and practical endeavor. All were level five.

Then she added, "There are two things I saw in you that drew me to you. First, I saw how hard you were willing to work. Second, I saw that you were very intelligent." We both cried. I thought, "Do saints weep?" and I answered, "Christine does."

At every church we served, she stood by my side. She taught Sunday School. She sang in the choir. She went to women's groups, even though that was not her favorite thing to do. She sat with our boys as I led worship. When I came home broken from many disappointments, she comforted me. When I was not sure I had made the right decision, we would talk and pray it out.

Her love and loyalty kept me going when there were times I really wanted to quit. She even helped me see that people could be different and still be very spiritual persons.

This made me more sensitive to people who had got themselves into real messes. There was the poor woman who was obviously being over medicated. I negotiated with her doctor to look for another approach, and he did. This was inspired by my Chrissy's courage in confronting her own superiors.

After four years of teaching, she entered the field of rehabilitation of the mentally ill and developmentally disabled. So often, she had to fight against the very people who had hired her to get the proper care for the handicapped that would help them be more independent. Many of the workers she supervised thought they were being helpful if they did much more than was needed for the clients. She helped them see that they weren't really helping them. Some of her superiors had to be shown a better way as well.

Then there was the woman who appealed to me to go visit her dying brother, Robert. Robert was still a member of the church I was serving, but I had never met him. His family attended the church but Robert had ceased attending years before. Robert had become or had recognized his homosexuality and had years before decided to lead that kind of life. He had contracted aids and was within days of life's end.

Robert, although about six feet tall, was emaciated and was then weighing less than one hundred pounds. We spoke for as long as he wished to talk. I think it was over an hour. I recognized my own need for continued healing, even as I recognized his need. We even laughed over some of the unusual things that had happened in each of our lives over the years. Mostly we spoke of God's love, which was for all people in any situation.

The feeling of both God's love and my wife's love was tangible in that room. We prayed together, and I prayed God's healing and salvation for him. He confessed his sins and shortcomings and surrendered to God's loving embrace. We embraced, and then he laid back on the bed. Before I could get to the hospital to see him again, his sister told me that he had died. We conducted his funeral in the church, and I was able to tell his family and the assembled congregation that Robert had received God's saving grace while we were visiting.

We are surrounded by saints. Saints are in this world and in the next. Is there really that much difference between here and there? The communion of saints was expanding in my soul and was expanding my soul. It was allowing me to be the kind of minister I had always wished to be. The only stagnation was the drag produced by my failure to compete for my dissertation. However, if generativity means producing children to become worthwhile adults and fulfilling a vocation, then God was healing my soul in ways that were wonderful.

In the next chapter, we will examine my movement into stage seven, the generative stage.

Chapter 7

PRODUCTIVITY VS. STAGNATION

"Universal Salvation"

"I don't eat meat except for hamburgers."

—A practicing Hindu in a McDonald's Restaurant

Before I move to the next stage of psychosocial development, I must address how I began to discover what was important to hold firmly and what was possible to modify, in this stage, Erikson called the generative or productive stage. As Erikson opined, "the mature man needs to be needed."[23]

I claim to be balding because I scratch my head so much over the strange inconsistencies I've encountered over the years. Perhaps that's the reason, but when I encountered a family, I knew to be practicing members of the religion rightly called *Sanatana Dharma*, the ancient teaching, in a McDonald's, consuming hamburgers, I asked them why they did that. I was mostly just curious, but the answer began a serious question of how seriously one should take one's teaching in order to remain what one claims to be. The mother answered, "We are vegetarians. We don't eat meat except for hamburgers." We both smiled at each other and went about our business. This was a fine family, but I wondered why one would claim to follow a teaching if one doesn't actually follow it.

This became a serious issue when the last mainline protestant bishop under whom I served in active ministry openly questioned some basic teachings of the Christian Church. Should I find a way to support him in some way? Or should I retire and openly challenge him?

It mattered because I had thought through the issues and found the best explanation for the healing of the soul was found in Christian teaching. I even understood that many, if not most of these truths, were taught in other ways not only in all branches of Christianity but in most if not all of the world's religions. To a great degree, I had no problem with the many varieties in other religions. I didn't believe that I had to sacrifice truth for peace nor peace for truth.

One Protestant group might firmly state that Christ died to forgive all of our sins—past, present, and future—but another group might believe that a person could backslide. I understood the difference between the universal sacrifice of the cross and the vagaries of working out one's salvation with fear and trembling. I understood how the Holy Spirit worked with different people in different ways and that God could heal, who He and they chose to heal. I even wrote a college paper and two graduate-level papers on the subject. What I could not understand was how a leader of a religion would deny the very basic teachings of the religion that paid his salary and supported him. It made no sense. It seemed hypocritical and pointed to a lack of virtue and an abundance of hubris. Honestly, it should cause the person doing that to leave the group that he was pretending to lead.

A family eating hamburgers in a land and culture into which they are trying to fit into is one thing. A bishop who has vowed to defend and promote the teachings of the universal Church is and instead attacks those teachings is quite another.

Despite my growing doubts about that denomination's loyalty to saving the world, my struggle with it was causing me to have serious fits of depression. I found myself getting physically ill over some of the controversies in our conference, mainly centering on the cavalier approach the bishop and his cabinet were taking towards historic Christian teaching. My depression went so far as to consider suicide. God and my beloved Chrissy pulled me through.

What exactly did the bishop teach that threw me into such a quandary?

The last bishop I served proclaimed that the Trinity and the divinity of Christ are simply metaphors pointing to something else. It's as if he were to say the entire teachings of the Church are just cute stories that really have no objective meaning unless one wishes them to have meaning. Such a proclamation by a layperson might be forgiven out of ignorance but not from a bishop.

In fact, during my last appointment as an active pastor before retirement, I touched upon the truth of the Trinity. It is the first and most important teaching of the universal Christian Church. The depth of the teaching is beyond our full comprehension. It is a divine mystery, but it is the single most important teaching of the Christian Church. An older member of the Church I had grown to love dearly asked me with surprise in his voice and on his face, "Do you mean that Jesus Christ is also God?"

So, it's not surprising that when the opportunity arose, I challenged the bishop with two questions: If the Trinity and the Divinity of Christ are simply metaphors to what do they refer? We don't worship figures of speech, nor do we teach people that what we believe at the heart of life are simply figures of speech. Why should we not teach that burning leaves will bring about salvation and healing of souls if these are just metaphors? He had no answer for that challenge.

The second question was not as important at the time for me, but since I had studied the ancient Church I asked it. How is this teaching any different from the teachings of heretics against the accepted teachings of the Church? Specifically, how is this teaching that Christ is not divine, and the Trinity is only a metaphor any different from what he taught? I mentioned that Arius the heretic taught this, but also other heretical groups like the Monophysites (Miaphysites) and the Nestorians taught this as well. These positions were all condemned by the early Church. His answer was simply to deflect the question by commenting, "Well, which heresy are you charging me with?"

No other bishop openly challenged him. I could not understand or tolerate this.

I retired from that Church in my early fifties because my

conscience, which is a function of my soul, could not defend a Church that taught its basic teachings meant so little for the healing of the world. The healing or saving of the world is the Church's primary purpose. "For God so loved the world that he gave his only begotten Son that whosoever believes in Him should not perish but have eternal life" (John 3:16).

Now I was struggling with a problem that was similar to the one I faced when I failed to complete my dissertation. How does a man provide for his family, though our children were gone, and not have a vocation? It was easier than the dissertation issue in the sense that we had some savings, but complicated by the fact that I was no longer young. I had followed the pathway of integrity but still struggled with despair.

Many options stood before me. Should I go to some denomination that would let me start a church from scratch? But what denomination? I had pretty much decided that most denominations did not respect the historical Church any more than the one I was leaving.

How about high school teaching? I would need to teach something for which I was qualified. No matter how well educated I was, I knew very little about the hoops I must confront in order to be certified by the state. More than that, I knew enough about public education theory to know that much of it was more bureaucracy than I was ready to tolerate.

One day my bride and I decided to get the holiness part of our lives in order first and then see where God would lead us. Suddenly the issue became clear "we must go to the Church that has existed since the life of Jesus and the Apostles. That narrowed our decision to either the Orthodox or the Catholic Church. Almost all that I knew of either was my graduate studies at Garrett and Northwestern, which was focused upon the Fathers of the Church with some medieval studies.

After some searching, we walked into a newly built temple that at first looked like a mosque. It was very sparse except for a giant lovely painting of a woman holding a child in front of her. I knew what this was from my studies but I had never seen it before, and in the center of the ceiling, I saw a very large picture of Christ Almighty with a book held in the bend of his left arm and holding up His hand in the sign of a blessing. I noticed the sweet smell of incense, and I knew that God had led us here.

I was so certain of this that the ancient refrain uttered first by Samuel's mother, Hanna, and by Mary, the mother of Jesus the Christ.

> *"My soul doth magnify the Lord, And my spirit hath rejoiced in God my Saviour" kept ringing in my heart and in my mind.*

Wherever I was to go from here, I knew that I was home.

> *The very shape of the Temple spoke to my soul that the fulfillment that Christ "will put everything under His feet" and somehow, it was related to this reality. It was a domed shaped temple, which looked as if heaven had come down to bring me up. I remembered the famous comment from most famously Saints Irenaeus and*

> *Athanasius but throughout the Fathers of the Church that "God became man that we might become God."*[24]

In a strange way, the Hindu-family-eating-hamburgers made some sense to me. God had come even to Hindus not to have them eat hamburgers but to reach them where they are.

I remembered the passage from St. John's Gospel that was uttered by St. John the Baptist upon seeing Christ come to him in the Jordan Valley "He is the true light that enlightens everyone, who is now coming into the world" (John 1:9).

I had often wondered how it was that people of seemingly different religions could be so kind and generous. I even wondered how it could be that people who believed themselves to be atheists were otherwise so full of what I perceived God to be.

Is it possible that God works through those He chooses to work through, and His actions are not subject to my determination? Is it possible that people I had been taught were not saved were actually being saved in ways I could not fully comprehend? Was it possible that the final step in the healing of my soul came by way of my call to holiness at thirteen years old at a protestant holiness camp meeting? Was it possible that it led through my education at small rural schools than through a university and seminary that taught me more than I ever thought possible? Could this step to a church that seemed to combine all of that in a setting that came from the heavens to me, and brought me up to meet Him be the perspective that my soul needed for its greatest step in this life? I seemed to be perched on a platform that helped me see things a little closer to how God saw things.

Mix that in with Jesus' own words, "I have sheep not of this fold" John 10:16 and His unusual word about the Holy Spirit who like the wind "blows where He wills, and you hear the sound of it, but you do not know whence it comes or whither it goes; so it is with everyone who is born of the Spirit" (John 3:8). On that day, I was again "born of the Spirit" in a new way.

The medicine for the soul began to show me that healing and salvation were much bigger than simply one soul being rescued out of a group of people. For a person's soul to be truly healed and made whole, one must know the truth that one must indeed "follow peace with all men and holiness without which no one will see the Lord" (Hebrews 12:14). I knew the words of that passage, but I never knew of the depth of that reality, and if truth be told, this is not something that can ever be fully grasped. "The completely healed soul is one that becomes one with God" (I Corinthians 15: 27-28) and "continues to grow from glory unto glory" (2 Corinthians 3:18). "Why else would people pray for the dead?" (I Corinthians 15:29). "Why else would people proclaim the communion of the saints?" (Apostles' Creed and Hebrews 12). "Why else would people know that the saints pray for us?" (Rev 5-7). Let's explore the teachings of the fathers of the Church. Let's explore the teachings of those who were closest to the apostles and prophets. I had studied them years before, but now I had a much better context for understanding them.

Chapter 8

FOUNDATIONS: TERTULLIAN AND ORIGEN

"The Life of the Body is the Soul.
The life of the Soul is God."
—St. Anthony of Padua

"Only one life 'twill soon be past.
Only what's done for Christ will last."
—Charles Studd

This note on my grandparents' front door was something I have thought about since I knowingly first responded to the call of Christ at age thirteen.

I wondered if the actions I took for Christ would somehow affect others? I wondered if the actions I took would somehow affect me? If these actions are to last, how long would they last?

Is there a time limit to how long they would last? If Christ lives forever, why would there ever be an end to the effects they had? If those questions could somehow be answered, then what does it mean that we only have one life, and it will soon be past? Is there nothing done in this life that has any continuing value beyond this particular physical life? How long will the one life last? Is this one life measurable? If there is a life after this physical existence, as the Church tells us, how long does this one life last? Should we be so prideful that we would think that this one life only began in this physical life if, in fact, it could go on forever? If this life could go on forever ahead of us, why should we not think that the soul did not precede this particular physical manifestation of it? Then if the soul can belong to Christ, why should we ever think that it does not exist forever without limit? If the soul continues beyond this physical life, where does it exist? Is it possible that what is called purgatory is simply a way of understanding a cleansing or purging while in possession of other bodies?

As a callow youth, I wondered if I was the only one who thought of these things?

It didn't matter what I was doing; I would wonder about these things. When the teacher spoke, I would think about these things. What difference does it make when someone expresses some great discovery? Does this insight last beyond the teacher? Was this insight made by others prior to this person's insight? I thought about these questions when the preacher would talk about heaven or repentance or learning to do good things.

When still in elementary school, on hot summer nights, my

mother would suggest that we all go outside and look up at the stars and try to count them. I would try to imagine how far away these stars were from us. We understood that occasionally we could even catch a glimpse of a planet like earth. Sometimes we would read that Venus or Mars could be seen in relation to the moon. We would scan the skies to see if we could find them. We found the Big Dipper and the Little Dipper and could follow them to the North Star. I wonder now if some of Einstein's insights came first by contemplating the stars as a child. I didn't know anything about Einstein, but I was beginning to think about things that have remained with me all of my life.

These thoughts came to me when I began the study of two of my favorite Christian authors. In fact, they remained with me when I encountered thinkers, even outside the Christian faith. For now, we shall discuss the two authors that were foundational thinkers for both Western and Eastern Christianity: Tertullian of Carthage and Origen of Alexandria.

This may seem like a detour from the direction of this book. Quentin Tarantino has made a living by moving back and forth in time to pick up a thread. So, I will pick up a thread from my earlier studies, which formed the basis for subsequent investigations. I now wish to express my move from Tertullian's view of strict conversions in the present life or destruction in the next to a view more influenced by Origen's reflections upon restoration and universal salvation.

Tertullian is considered to be the father of Latin Christianity. Latin Christianity is a common way of speaking about Christianity that originally came from Christianity centered in Rome. The Catholicism that most people in Europe or the Western Hemisphere understand to be Catholicism and all of Christianity that comes from the Protestant Reformation or Revolution. He established how questions like the Trinity would be discussed in Latin Christianity even until today when he dismantled Marcion in five books. *Adversus Marcionem* (*Against Marcion)* Additionally, when he wrote about the Soul in *De Anima,* he set the standard for Latin thinking on the subject. While his comments set his thoughts apart from previous philosophical ideas, his insistence that individual souls were made at conception of the physical individual remains today the principle way of discussing the soul in Latin thought.

At the end of this physical life, the soul is rewarded or punished or disappears, but little is discussed about what is considered to be speculative matters. And very little is discussed about what is commonly called the afterlife. In the process, Tertullian rejected all philosophical approaches that dealt with the afterlife or the continued life of the soul.

Tertullian's greatest contribution concerning the understanding of the soul was his sense of how the corruption of the human soul was passed on to all of humanity. Tertullian was a materialist. He spoke of the soul as corporeal. It follows that the soul and its corruption are passed on through procreation. This understanding is called *Traducianism*, which is that its reality is passed on through the physical action of procreation.

Tertullian was a lawyer by training, and this had a large impact upon his thinking. In any event, Western Christianity to this day discusses the afterlife and questions considered speculative, much less than does Eastern Christianity and instead focuses upon determining forensic definitions.

The East had and has a more robust approach to such matters but avoided and avoids the tendency of the West to limit discussions to this life. Justin Martyr, for example, did not hesitate to discuss the value of pagan philosophy but insisted that they had forsaken some of the better parts of it.[25] Even today, there are icons of people like Plato and Aristotle inside Orthodox Churches because their thinking was understood to be reflective of Christ's influence even prior to Christ's incarnation.[26]

So, we come to the thinker in the East who was, and I would contend, is most influential of Greek thought on this matter, Origen of Alexandria. Redemption of all of creation is summarized with the use of the term Apokatastasis. It is common in the writings of the church fathers.[27] The basic translation of the term is restoration. This refers to the ultimate restoration of all souls back to God from whom we came. This could ultimately include even Satan and the fallen angels, which is predicated on the doctrine of reincarnation, similar to karma.

In this view, the soul has been harmed and is incomplete. Earthly life is a remedy for prenatal sin. The soul only becomes complete as it is finally healed and reunited with God.

In other words, God created the soul not as an essence but as a possibility. The possibility is that the souls will be reunited through holy living with God. When the soul comes freely to the recognition of God's love, it becomes completed through restoration into the Being of God.[28]

This reuniting that heals the inherited disease of the soul and unites us with God through holy living is called Theosis. It is the participation in the divine nature. It is also called deification.[29]

The point of restoration is to return all that had fallen back to God, even the author of the fall, Lucifer.

Origen taught that souls pre-existed the bodies that they were to fill. Before the foundation of the world (Ephesians 1:4), we were chosen in Him. These souls, though they fell, were to be restored in bodies that were as holy as they were when created. All will eventually, in God's time, be restored to the position God created and intends for all. None are to be lost because of the work of Jesus Christ.

The parable of the lost sheep from Luke 15:4-5, "What man of you, having a hundred sheep, if he has lost one of them, does not leave the ninety-nine in the wilderness, and goes after the one which is lost, until he finds it? And when he has found it, he lays it on his shoulders, rejoicing."[30] This is the assurance that God will never abandon anyone. Through Christ, everyone and everything will be made whole.[31]

These ideas have had a tremendous impact on me and my approach to the lost. It became more and more clear to me that it's God's business to save and heal. His intention is to do just that. Nothing will stop His intentions from completion. It is also clear that while the "Lord adds daily, those who are being saved." Acts 2:47 It is also the responsibility of those who are being saved to witness to the whole world the salvation that God has purchased for them and to teach and baptize wherever we are, as it is recorded in Jesus' words in Matthew 28:19–20. This freed me to approach my vocation of evangelism, exhortation, and pastoring with much more compassion and kindness than if, on the one hand, I thought it my responsibility to save others and on the other that God was interested in condemning anyone.

It moved me to want to work with the confused and lost. It moved me to help our church start a food pantry. It moved me to pray and listen to people caught in all kinds of sins. It moved me to pray for those who were in need.

During my first pastoral assignment, rumblings of unrest started among our city's police department and the city's trustees in Worth, Illinois. There were rumors of an imminent blue flu.

The two groups had tried to work out their labor differences for several months, but several intractable issues remained. What could this possibly have to do with a pastor's work? Why should a pastor have anything to do with such matters? If I had not been aware of the idea of restoration or had interpreted the Lord's Prayer differently, I would have shrugged my shoulders and pretty much ignored the issue. I may have, but events and I believe God intervened.

Didn't our Lord pray, "Thy will be done on earth as it is in heaven"? Was God interested in the trouble that would come about if the Trustees and the police, both made up of well-intentioned people, could not reach an agreement? Had God called me into ministry without equipping me with the ability to shed some light from God and his heavenly city to this earthly city? I thought to the contrary that I had been given the light of Christ that could be shed upon this city and upon its brokenness.

One day the mayor and the police chief came to see me. I knew that they had contacted the pastor of the largest church in the city for help with this labor and budgetary problem and had been turned down. I wondered why they were coming to see the youngest pastor in town, of a relatively small church. They told me that the state budget requests were to be submitted in a week, and the two groups were at an impasse over certain issues, including wage issues.

Here I was, only a lowly Deacon. In our denomination, that meant I had not yet been ordained a Presbyter, or as it is called, Elder. After switching from the PhD program, I was still in seminary. Who was I that the city leaders would ask me for help? By what I believed to be providence, I was taking a course in the theological ramification of "City Planning." After learning some of the issues, I took the assignment. I was part of fulfilling the Lord's Prayer. Didn't He say, "Thy will be done on earth as it is in heaven." Moreover, if God was restoring all things to Himself wasn't this part of that restoration.

Before our first meeting, I asked for the documents from both groups. When I received over three feet of documents, I knew I would never be able to cut through all of that, but with consultation with my professor, I knew I did not need to read through all of these papers. That wasn't what I was to do.

Here's what I was led to do. On the night before the budget was to be sent to Springfield, I called all the representatives from both the police and city hall to meet at my church. This was holy work, and I wanted them to take this seriously.

We began with prayer. I then listed the issues on the newsprint that both groups agreed with and ranked their priority. I then divided them into Sunday School rooms. Starting with the lowest priority items, which would be the easiest to solve, I went back and forth between the two rooms until the two sides had agreed upon solutions to all of the issues except for salaries. We had started at seven p.m. It was then three a.m., and we had reached an impasse. It seemed we were about to fail when the police chief said, "Pastor Lauffer has sacrificed so much to see this resolved. We cannot stop now. We cannot let him down." God is good. All the time.

We went back to work and reached a final agreement about 4:30 a.m. The budget was sent to the capital. The strike was averted.

I felt strangely renewed and revived. I felt closer to God than I had in a long time. I knew that working to bring us to follow peace and holiness that my own soul was being healed.

About a year later, the bishop moved me to another assignment. The church, the city board, and the police put on a wonderful party for my wife and I, and gave us a plaque commemorating my work with them.

God desires to restore all things to Himself. He wants us all to follow peace with all and holiness without which no one will see the Lord. My soul, that is I, was continuing to be healed.

If what seems to be the case, then someday in God's time, we will all be restored to Him. My sense is to make this task as easy on God and on myself as I could, and so I will try to follow peace and holiness. My hope is that someday I will see all my loved ones together with God in the Marriage Supper of the Lamb.

Now we move onto another aspect of generativity as I reflect upon our children.

Chapter 9

GENERATIVITY AND CHILDREN

"The soul is healed by being with children."

—Fyodor Dostoyevsky

"It's easier to build strong children, than to repair broken men."

—Frederick Douglass

I kept trying to find a way to complete my dissertation but finally gave up and decided to turn my attention to my first real calling, that of pastoral ministry.

Before switching back to that, another primary calling came knocking. My beloved greeted me one day with a big smile on her face. I remember the date quite well for the summer was hot, and the seminary air conditioning was inadequate. But that was not why she was smiling.

She handed me a bottle of pills with the date July 7, 1977. That's 7777. Since we both were trained and loved religious symbolism, I knew that something very important was happening. I glanced down and noticed that the cost of the medicine was $7.77. If that wasn't enough, the bottle contained prenatal vitamins. Then she handed me a single recording by Paul Anka titled "Having your Baby." I swept her up in my arms and cried aloud with joy. In fact, we both did.

A tiny fear, which I was ready to dismiss, niggled at my brain. Will I be a better father than my father was? But for that moment, I brushed the thought away.

As my wife's stomach became larger and larger, I was ever more grateful for her willingness to go through this. She loved being pregnant. She loved the attention and loved the fact that a life was growing within her.

Then the days arrived. After a couple of Braxton Hix false labors, in which she was admitted and her contractions stopped. Then the real thing came. Since we took Lamaze training together, I was with her the whole time. I rubbed her back. I helped her breathe properly. After several hours she was given Pitocin to move the delivery along. When the baby came, I named him after my first American-born ancestor, and after my middle name. Christian Daniel was an absolute delight.

There was one problem. I was sure that my wife and I had agreed upon the name, but my good wife reminded me that we had not. But she just smiled and said, "it's a good name."

One day when Christian was only a few weeks old, I tossed him up a bit further than I had intended but breathlessly prayed for his safety as I caught him. I was learning how to show joy without doing damage to our little guy by almost hurting him.

When Christian was three, we discovered that Andrew David was on the way. The labor was much easier. I barely got to the hospital before he was born.

Shortly after Andrew's birth, my wife's mother came down to help with things the first few days, and I took Christian to a cabin for a few days to show that he remained special in our estimation. During that period, it became clear to me that I enjoyed being a father and would probably do a pretty good job of it.

When both of our sons turned five, we decided to enroll them in Suzuki violin. This required one of us to oversee their practice and to go with them to their lessons. We chose Suzuki because it allows students to learn to play music even before they could read it. That's a very natural pattern and one that was helpful for Daddy, who could not really read music either. When asked what musical instrument I played, I would always say, "the radio." Ah, but I loved being with our sons and helping them learn to listen to and to play beautiful music.

When Christian was still five, he and I went to our first concert. The program started with more advanced violinists, and as the compositions grew more simply played, and Christian had not gone up to the platform to join the others, I leaned over to him and asked, "Won't it be wonderful to play just like those students do?" He answered without missing a beat, "I already do." Which of course was right, and the exchange gave me another sermon illustration on sanctification or the "healing of the soul" as I later came to understand it.

Every person who seeks consciously or unconsciously to become whole or attempts to be the very best one can at every stage of life is experiencing the healing of the soul. My son taught me a wonderful lesson on how to be a dad, or in Erikson's terms, he taught me a lesson is generativity. My soul was, indeed, being healed.

Of course, this proud father rejoiced when his son joined the others and played the most beautiful rendition of "Twinkle, Twinkle, Little Star" I had ever heard.

Our second son presented new challenges, not least of which was how he was born. He came more quickly than his brother, and his dad almost missed his birth. That story is for the next chapter but let me tell you a bit about Andy.

Andy was what people called "big boned." While three and a half years younger than his brother, he knew how to protect himself physically and was actually bigger than most of the children his age in the earliest years of school. Frequently the teacher would ask us for a conference. Invariably the comment was, "he intimidates the other children." We'd ask, "Has he ever attacked them or hurt them?" "No," was always the answer. "Actually, he is so eager to join in that he frightens the others." This turned out to be to his great advantage when he played a lineman in high school football years later. It also was an advantage when his older, taller brother would tease him. Andy could usually handle himself with his brother.

On at least two occasions, Andy, the younger, rescued his older brother. The neighbor boy, who was older and heavier than Christian, started to pick on both Andy and Christian.

He was getting the better of Christian when Andy leaped upon the neighbor kid's back and began to pummel him. The battle ended when the neighbor boy, probably astonished at Andy's chutzpa, left the field.

On another occasion, we were camping in the Smoky Mountains when Andy came running to me, calling out for me to come and save Christian. Christian had tried to climb over a fence but caught his leg on a protruding wire. I proudly saved him and expressed admiration to Andy for his quick action.

I was also learning how to generate myself in how I was learning to be a father who was different from my own.

From college days, I recall reading the works of Plato and Aristotle and their thoughts on the gymnasium. There was a need for an adult male to guide the young men. Today it is popular to imagine inferences to pedophilia in certain circles. Those were not discussed in my study. Nevertheless, my sons needed a father, and I was very interested in being a good one. The gymnasium combined physical fitness with the learning of math, philosophy, religion, and the arts. This appealed to me as a natural pattern for working with our sons.

I also found a balance in this approach, which is reflected not only in Aristotle's *Golden Mean,* but in the Buddhist's Middle Way. One Socratic dialogue has the great philosopher and mentor of Plato saying of the Mean: "It is a conjunction of three: beauty, proportion, and truth. Let us affirm, these should be treated as a unity and be held responsible for what is in the mixture, for goodness is what makes the mixture good in itself" (Plato, *Philebus*, 64d–65a).

My standard was that each of our sons would be encouraged to participate in one artistic endeavor, one sport, and to do their best in the academic training afforded them in public school. We attended summer arts camps, both boys took Suzuki violin lessons, and played sports. Christian loved soccer and basketball, and Andy loved football.

I also found great joy in working with Andy on the violin. He never got to play the instrument as often as his older brother since the bishop moved me out of the Chicago area and away from any Suzuki academy, but he was always a good performer. During one performance at a summer camp for the arts, Andy was so absorbed in his very fine performance that upon completion, he bowed not to the audience but to the wall. He never realized that he had. Andy was so focused on doing well that he didn't notice other things.

Andy and the principal had a friendship I learned about in a surprising way. The principal indicated that he enjoyed his almost daily discussions with Andy. "When do these discussions happen," I asked? "Near the beginning of the school days," he responded. "He arrives late almost every day, and he's sent to my office." Before I could explain our dilemma, he said, "Don't worry. I understand what's going on, and actually, I learn a great deal from him, and I hope he learns some things from me. Andy is from an urban setting, and he really does not enjoy being here. I am in the same situation. This is my first assignment as a principal small town, and I will be glad when it's over." Andy had found a way to learn in a setting in which he could learn. Perhaps we were on the right track to send him to an elementary school that used the Montessori principles of individual learning. The principal went on to his next assignment the same year we left the rural town.

Christian traveled to Europe three times with the high school orchestra. We paid for his first trip, but he paid for the second and third.

One day this schedule blew up in a fairly minor way during the days he was working, attending school, and saving for his trip. It was quite common that my workday at the church began at eight a.m. but did not end until nine or ten at night. I came home about nine p.m. and was greeted at the door by my wife and Christian.

Chris seemed perplexed when she told me, "Christian sassed me today. I did not know what to do and told him that, but that we would let him know the consequence for his behavior later. Christian was seventeen with a schedule that, at his age, was too much. He was taking rather advanced courses, working part-time, and playing in an orchestra. While keeping that schedule, he was making almost straight A's.

Chris and I talked about this together and decided that there was nothing we could take away from him as a consequence. We couldn't ground him from anything. He was too busy with things he had to do for there to be anything useful from which to ground him. We wondered if a ban on TV would be a good thing, but he did not watch TV.

We decided together that he was overwhelmed with his responsibilities and hadn't had any fun things in his life for some time.

I reached into my billfold and pulled out a $20.00 bill. I took out a piece of paper on which I wrote the following: "Dear Christian, you are a good son, but you have sassed your mother. We know that you are trying to keep a schedule that is almost overwhelming. Therefore, your consequence is that you must take this $20.00 and go out with your friends and relax. With Love, your Mom and Dad." He read the note. His eyes got big. A tear began to flow. He hugged his mom and apologized.

The way I was led to discipline our sons showed me again that despite my father's angry and violent way he treated his wife and children, I did not need to do that. I was becoming a better father than my father, as Oedipus had hoped for himself.

Both Christian and Andrew had successful college careers, and both are married with lovely children and good jobs.

My wife and I pray for and rejoice over what God has allowed us to see in our children. My own soul is continually being healed because I am fulfilling, with God's help, the generative stage of my life in wonderful ways.

I have learned to pray for my mom and dad that God will show mercy on them, and given that God is not dependent upon time, and perhaps they are or will be praying for my soul. I do not know these things. As the saying goes, "such knowledge is above my pay scale." Even better, "God's ways are not our ways." The Psalmist wrote, "I praise Thee, for Thou art fearful and wonderful. Wonderful are Thy works."

Erikson calls this the seventh stage of development, which we are calling here the healing of the soul. He summarizes this as he transitions to the eighth and final stage this way: "Only in those who have taken care of things and people and have adapted themselves to the triumphs and disappointments adherent to being the originator of others and or the generator of products and ideas . . . only in him may gradually ripen the fruit of the seven stages of ego integrity."[32]

Reflecting back upon my experience with my own father, I realize that his mentorship had positive aspects and some positive results. I learned the importance of every member of every family. I spent most of my time outside of school, helping my father in various ways in his small business. If I had not, the family would not have survived economically and barely did even with my father's utilization of me. At the time, I often resented not having much free time, but I learned the value of hard work and honesty from my father, and I was able to pass on those lessons to our sons.

I am content with a few small exceptions about which I will reflect upon later that "our originator of others" stage regarding rearing children is going well. Now onto the "generator of products and ideas" period will be analyzed.

Chapter 10

GENERATIVITY PART 2

"He is an abscess on the universe who withdraws and separates himself from the reason of our common nature through being displeased with the things which happen, for the same nature that produces this, and has produced thee also . . ."

—Marcus Aurelius, *Meditations*

So, where was I when I nearly missed the birth of our second child? Before I explain this, let me give a little background.

The question then is, "how did I learn to follow peace with all and holiness without which no one shall see the Lord" when it comes to generating products and ideas.

I had not given it much thought while being protestant. In fact, Protestantism rarely addresses the topic. Most pastors were married, and single pastors were the exception. In any event, no one really raised the issue of whether or not a pastor could be married both to a person of the opposite sex and married to the Church at the same time. But since we became part of an Eastern Catholic Church, I have had to reflect upon that. Eastern Catholics are Orthodox Christians, i.e., Eastern Christians by and large use an Orthodox liturgy and follow the praxis of the Orthodox, but at the same time are in communion with Rome. The default position of the Roman Catholic Church is not to ordain married men. The historical position in the Eastern Church is that many priests are married so long as they are married before they are ordained.

I was, or more precisely, I am a married pastor in the retired status. We worked as a team all of our married life. I was able to merge the two parts of the vocation by seeing marriage as the overriding sacrament, as I was to learn later in life. The image of heaven as the "marriage supper of the Lamb" is an expression that defines all Christians as forever married to all other Christians. The marriage of a man and a woman is the same marriage between a priest and the Church. In fact, that is the meaning of Ephesians 5:25:

> *"Be subject to one another out of reverence for Christ . . . This is a great mystery, and I am applying it to Christ and the church. Each of you, however, should love his wife as himself, and a wife should respect her husband."*

When arriving at my first full-time appointment as an ordained deacon, I immediately noticed that the attendance was very low based upon the number of members registered, and 80% of those in attendance were women, and most of them were over fifty. That's not eighty women and twenty men, but thirty-two women and eight men. God bless the women, but that means that we not only had few women but almost no men. It also meant, as I discovered very soon, we had virtually no families with children. A couple of families came occasionally but not regularly. Why would they? There was nothing much there for them.

About a couple of months in, I decided to take the bull by the horns. I stood before the congregation and challenged them to have a Sunday School. "We need six teachers for six classes, and I believe we will get them before we continue the worship service." I'm not sure, but I think the people believed that their pastor cared about their church and their families because within five minutes after the sermon we had filled the slots. I also think they believed that their pastor was a little crazy but, in their kindness, they would humor me.

A few weeks later, I tackled the next problem. We had no nursery. Why should we, people probably thought, when we have no families with babies. Still, I stood before the congregation and challenged them to give $2,000 to remodel a room for such a purpose. I warned them not to scratch their noses unless they were pledging toward the project. Chris and I had agreed ahead of time that we would pledge $200. So, I did. Within eight minutes after the sermon, we had the $2,000 pledged, and within a few weeks, we had a cry room.

By the second year, we were having a regular attendance of over ninety with about thirty men and sixty women. Most of our new members and returning members were families with children. During my final year at this first appointment, we averaged 110 with about 40% male and 60% female attendance.

What happened during those twenty-seven years as a pastor? Of course, there were some tough times, but I loved those years too. So often, God put people in my life that I could help. I met low-income men and women and directed them to employment, and softened the transition through rental and food help. I met people who were disappointed over things that had happened to them, or what they themselves had done that brought them great sorrow. We helped struggling children and families. Many times, new people would say, "I wish I had been introduced to this before." I would often say, "God's timing is always right. Would you have been receptive before?"

One older couple shared the horrible death of their five-year-old son many years before. Many times, we prayed and talked. One evening we had an auction to support missions. A little red wheelbarrow came up for auction, and I was surprised how much money was bid for it. The winners of the auction had become friends with the owners of the wagon. When they won the wheelbarrow, they gave it to my wife and me for our young son. The couple who had owned it told me that it was one of the last things that their little son had owned. It was, as they explained, given this as an act of healing from their grief. We wept together as all of our souls were being healed that night.

The United Methodist Church has something they call apportionments. Apportionments were how the governing body apportioned the conference and mission expenses to each congregation. To my surprise, Worth Church had never paid their full apportionment. We did while I was their pastor. We did it by bringing missions alive to the church congregation. For the last three years as their pastor, we had monthly mission meetings, which contained food indigenous to the countries we featured, skits, and visiting speakers. We raised money for mission projects above and beyond the apportionments.

We were also successful in passing on a positive faith to children. The reviving of our emphasis upon families and children made our SS bulge with activity. One such activity was led by my beloved wife. It is called Bible Bowl. Bible Bowl trains the children in teachings from the Bible. The Bible Bowl has the Bible Boys and the Gospel Girls. It was so popular that a local TV station filmed it and broadcasted it. Worth Church was on the map again because we decided to increase the following.

We expanded our ministry by establishing a food pantry. We negotiated a settlement between the police and village hall. We helped city residents to establish a stable vision for the future of the city into the next several decades, which has come to fruition.

So, what was I doing the night our second son was born?

The very next summer, August 12, 1981, I decided to call a meeting of all interested citizens of the village to begin plans for the future of Worth, Illinois. The mayor again had approached me with the idea. Why not, was my immediate reaction.

We arranged to meet in the elementary school gymnasium for an evening of planning. I had learned and utilized a very effective program called "The Nominal Group Technique" which involved ways to give everyone the opportunity to share their ideas and then develop all of them into groups of program plans for the city.[33] It was to be a much more eventful night than I had realized.

Over 200 people from our town showed up. We had newspaper and Television coverage for the event. It was an enormous success.

Before the meeting began, my wife had gone into labor, and I took her to Christ Hospital in Oak Lawn, Illinois. We agreed that the baby would probably take a long time in his arrival as our first son had taken, so with much trepidation, I went to the meeting and led it. As soon as the meeting was over, I drove to the hospital, wondering all the time if I would make it back before our second was born. I was also worried about what my dear wife would think about my divided attention at this extremely important time.

As it turned out Andy, like Christian before him, came at his own time. He was a Pitocin baby, which means he wouldn't come without a medication that was designed to pretty much force him out. He did not come until 5:30 a.m. the next morning.

We saw the fruits of our labor, or my wife's labor to be more accurate, very quickly. However, by the next spring, the bishop had other plans for us, so that we were not able to see the fruit of our city planning. We have, however, seen it since. The main route through town is beautiful. The Railroad line now runs on a bridge over Harlem Avenue. New stores operate in the village, and a golf course is now situated along the Calumet River. All of these plans started with the meeting of the 200.

As the day approached on which the bishop ordained our

leaving, there was a great sadness in my heart. I desperately wished to see the growth of this community of Christians. We needed to expand our church building. I wanted to see more and more people in our church. I knew we would eventually need a new parsonage. I knew we either needed more parking or we would need to move. We had taken over the only city's food pantry and had expanded it.

But there were other plans, and at that point, I wanted to be faithful to the larger Methodist Church and to my bishop. Still my heart was heavy.

The congregation, and as it turned out, many people of the village organized a going away party for us. To our surprise and joy, we packed the fellowship hall and had many who could not be seated. The mayor and the village trustees were there as well as the chief of police and fire chief. The mayor gave us a plaque to show appreciation for what we had done.

God had healed my soul to the point that I knew we were productive in what God had helped us create and generative in giving us two wonderful sons and a healthy marriage.

But testing was right around the corner, which in the long run made us stronger. We were less successful in our next assignment, but we survived. After only a brief stay, we were sent to a large Church, Court Street United Methodist Church, as the minister of evangelization in the mid-sized city of Rockford, Illinois.

We founded two singles clubs and helped to bring in an annual average of seventy new members to the church. We organized a large Thanksgiving Dinner held in our church's fellowship hall with an average of 125 volunteers from seventeen different churches in the area and served over 1,000 homeless and low-income families and individuals. God, in His goodness, allowed us to do this for five years running. My heart was full of joy. This became an annual event for the five years we served.

Then the bishop called again and asked me to take over a struggling church that had dropped to only twenty-five people. This assignment allowed us to remain in our home in Rockford, which was a great blessing. As I've recounted before, we quickly increased average attendance to 125, including many new members.

In some ways, this was a wonderful time. A member from our church in Rockford took it upon himself to nominate me for two evangelism and church growth awards. He discovered that he was too late for me to receive either of these while I was still at Court Street Church, so he resubmitted them the following two years. It was wonderful to receive the Denman Award for Evangelism by the Conference, the regional oversight body, in 1990 and then the following year to receive the Circuit Rider award for church growth by the entire denomination. Both were received for my work at Court Street and for my work at Harlem.

By 1992 the bishop called again and moved us to a North Shore church in Northbrook, Illinois. It should have been the best of times, but it wasn't. As it turned out, it wasn't the worst of times either.

Ultimately, I retired early to go seek another pattern of ministry and to seek peace with all and holiness without which no one would see the Lord. What that final stage would be, I did not know.

Ironically the final stage, according to Erikson, is the struggle between integrity and despair. Despair seems to always accompany the struggle for integrity. That last stage brings a sense of contentment. It was quite a struggle to reach it.

Would I continue to be generative in my career, or would I stagnate and collapse into despair?

Chapter 11

THE PENULTIMATE STEP:

Towards Ego Integrity over Despair

"Follow your bliss and the universe will open doors where there were only walls."

—Joseph Campbell

In Stage 8, Erikson discusses the final stage of this life. For those who understand that God is this is the final preparation of the soul for what we generally call the "afterlife." It may be better to describe it as the fulfillment of life.

The District Superintendent told me that my next appointment would probably be my last if I weren't successful. Maybe I should have said, "send me back to Worth," but I didn't. I had already tried to be transferred to Florida. I was tired of fighting what was called the Lifestyle issues and the then-popular worship of the goddess Sophia, which had been swirling around the Northern churches in Protestantism. Despite my successes and my recent awards, this could possibly be my last hurrah as an active Protestant minister.

Surprisingly, I wasn't particularly troubled. It wasn't that I didn't like ultimatums, put gently or not, but it was rather I was growing more and more weary of fighting heresy and more and more curious about the Church that has existed since Jesus and St. Peter. In other words, I was ambivalent about the appointment but willing to try.

My younger son was having difficulty in the Buffalo Grove schools. He was tested for a learning disability, but that didn't seem to be it. Christian had finished high school and was on his way to the University of Illinois. So, it seemed like a tolerable time to move.

I never really liked moving. Studies show that longer pastorates were better for the pastor as well as for the congregation, but I was willing to go.

Here I was in an interview for what turned out to be my last assignment before retirement. The question about the lifestyle issue came up. I gave them the official answer with which I easily agreed. "Every person is of sacred worth in God's eyes but . . ." but this particular practice "is incompatible with Christian teaching."[34] Our task will ever be to love all sinners into the kingdom, including myself, while not accepting practices that God says are wrong.

The problem was my last denominational bishop did not believe in this disciplinary standard, nor did he believe in the standard understanding of the Trinity or of the dual nature of

Jesus Christ. The bishop was openly hostile to the denominational and the standard Christian teachings.

When the denominational bishop began speaking out about how horrible the denomination was in their position on these topics and even led public protests against them, I spoke out against the bishop. When I spoke on the issue, I said that people who wish to change from disorder could be helped by the Church to change and forsake this disorder, and then I began hearing rumblings from some in the congregation. When the bishop, moreover, began describing the divinity of Christ and the Trinity as a mere metaphor, I made an appointment to speak with him privately. He graciously gave me his time, and I asked him what was the metaphor to which he referred? He had no clear answer. So, I pressed the issue "We do not worship figures of speech. We worship Christ as both divine and human, and we worship the Trinity. How is it that you say the one whom we worship is only a metaphor?" He simply repeated himself by saying our construction of it is only a metaphor. After listening to this in clergy sessions, I had enough.

His positions on Christ and the Trinity could not be ignored. I may have remained in the struggle for the denomination's stated position on the lifestyle issue, but I could not remain in a denomination that countenanced a position so clearly at odds with Christian doctrine as the dual nature of Christ and the Trinity.

I filed heresy charges against him, and another bishop came to Chicago to adjudicate the hearing. Two clergymen, myself and my friend, set out the case against the heretical positions that the bishop held and pronounced.

My charges weren't against him for his ordaining persons living an aberrant lifestyle. That was simply an action that offended discipline. Who knew what the discipline would be in the future? I filed heresy charges based upon his open stand against the divinity of Christ and against the doctrine of the Trinity.

Both before and after, I was not silent about my opposition to the bishop's actions and about my conflict with the bishop on these issues in both public conversation and even on occasion in sermons. I continued to explain who Jesus is and what the Trinity is. I continued to talk about the healing power of God to change one with disordered passions to ordered ones.

There was my problem. My soul wasn't fully healed. I know that the truth was not only what compelled me, but also my desire to be right and to convince others of it was causing trouble in my soul. I kept acting as if God's timing was not enough. I, too often, acted on my own will and not upon God's. Hence, I knew that I was not healed. I still needed to take that final step, whether in this life or the next. I still remained too self-conscious and too little God-conscious. Self-consciousness is merely the consciousness of this life and not of eternal life.

I was fighting with despair because I knew I had not yet reached a state of, in the words of Erikson, ego Integrity.[35]

In the words of St. Paul in Romans 7: 23:

> *"But I see another law in my members, warring against the law of my mind, and bringing me into captivity to the law of sin which is in my members. O wretched man*

> *that I am! Who shall deliver me from the body of this death? I thank God through Jesus Christ our Lord. So then with the mind I myself serve the law of God; but with the flesh the law of sin."*

I knew that I had not reached the point of integrity. One hasn't reached that stage if one is despairing about not having completed his work of generativity. I believed that if I lost this love-of-my-life vocation at this point, I was faced with stagnation. Yet I knew that once I had filed heresy charges against a bishop, I had no professional future in that denomination. I could retire and remain in a retired status. I would not lose my retirement, but I would be considered a pariah, at least among some bishops. A few would see me as a hero, but not that many. In any event, I would not get another active appointment, at least not from that bishop.

I entered the retirement status with a brief speech at the clergy session of the Annual Conference in June of 1999. In that speech, I thanked everyone for the opportunity to bring Christ to people and people to Christ. I remembered Robert, who surrendered to Christ in his last days of life. I remembered the family that reunited. I remembered all of the children and their families we had brought to Christ.

I remembered that I could not let go of the doctrinal problems that the bishop presented to the Church. Yes, the cause was righteous, but my ego attachment to it showed that my soul was not yet fully healed. I felt defeated but victorious at the same time.

Roberta Flack and Donny Hathaway transformed a beautiful hymn to a depth I had never heard in it before. Their song became my song during this period.

Come, ye disconsolate, where'er ye languish,
Come to the mercy seat, fervently kneel.
Here bring your wounded hearts, here tell your anguish;
Earth has no sorrow that heav'n cannot heal.

I wept many times and with bitter tears. I sought professional counseling. How could it be that I have done so much but now, entering the peak of my professional life, am I going to lose it all? Can it be that just as I received the greatest recognition of my professional life in the first two years of the 1990s. I was not ready to retire, especially under these circumstances.

I was indeed conflicted and certainly depressed. I was suffering.

Every religion in the world knows that suffering is universal. Buddhism has an interesting way to address this very real problem called the Four Noble Truths: Suffering (Dukkha) is universal; Suffering originates in our desires; Suffering will cease if all desires cease; and the way to realize this state is through the Eightfold Path. This state Buddhism calls Nirvana. It offers an excellent way and is not false.

However, Christianity adds one more element, which is fuller in most respects than Nirvana. Nirvana is primarily an absence of or an escape from reality. Christianity offers a more positive way by pointing to the example of Jesus Christ, who took suffering as a stepping-stone to unity with God.

St. Paul wrote or did use a hymn recorded in Philippians 2:5:

> *"Let the same mind be in you that was in Christ Jesus who, though he was in the form of God, did not regard equality with God as something to be exploited, but emptied himself, taking the form of a slave, being born in human likeness. And being found in human form, he humbled himself and became obedient to the point of death—even death on a cross."*

Luke records these words of Jesus when He was dying on the cross suffering the greatest humiliation possible, naked and defenseless, said of those murdering Him: Luke 23:34: "Father, forgive them; for they do not know what they are doing."

What one must do then is offer the suffering up to God.

In an analysis of the Psalms of King David, we find that 70% of the Psalms are complaints against God. We don't ignore the suffering, but we are to take our suffering to God. We are to "work out our own salvation with fear and trembling" (Philippians 2:12).

I'm not equal to the Apostles and not yet a saint. Therefore, it took me nearly a decade to learn those lessons.

I also knew that I could not defend what this bishop taught, nor could I defend the lack of outrage by other bishops over what that bishop was doing and teaching. My first step after retirement from active ministry had to be to find the Church that Jesus and the Apostles had inaugurated over 2000 years ago.

During the summer of 1999, my wife and I looked at each other after a brief prayer and concluded we must forsake all churches not founded on and by Christ. Our quest has always been to follow paths that would lead to holiness. Our next stop must be to an Orthodox or Catholic Church.

Chris had already moved ahead of me from our rural parish when she found a position in the mental health field at a very good agency near Chicago. They were open to her strong administrative abilities and her creative programmatic ideas. She was a wonderful match. She began her position in January 1999 and lived in a motel room while I finished my work at my last active appointment, and Andy finished high school there. We found housing in Joliet, Illinois, in a two-bedroom condo, and Chris joined me.

We looked at an Orthodox Church just before I moved from my rural assignment. It was a beautiful liturgy. It was a place I could find great joy and fulfillment. Would I be ordained in the Orthodox Church? The priest assured me that I would. The beauty of the liturgy, the faithfulness of Orthodoxy, and the promise of a future vocation were pleasing to hear. The answer to my final question was a disappointment. I asked, what is the possibility that at some point the Orthodox and the Catholics would find union, he said, "No possibility. No Orthodox priest even gives it a serious thought."

So, our search continued.

We had no Church, and I had no job.

Finally, we learned of a thing called an Eastern Catholic Church. We were told that it was, actually as it turns out they were, churches that were self-governed but in full communion with Rome. This sounded very promising. After some searching, we found the Byzantine Catholic Church in what became the village of Homer Glen, Illinois. We walked into the brand-new temple and smelled the incense, and saw two of what was to become several icons. I knew that we had come home.

This was where I was where my soul would be healed. Here is where I was to take a further step in my sometimes joyful, sometimes struggling, walk of holiness.

Still, I had no job. Men are supposed to provide for their families. I tried working with an insurance and financial planning company. I got many licenses. I tried selling funeral planning. Along with that, I was able to become an adjunct faculty member both at Joliet Junior College and at the University of St. Francis.

I taught courses in history, theology, philosophy, and world religions. For the most part, I enjoyed the experiences, but at five to seven courses a term it was sometimes exhausting.

In the midst of all of this, we started buying rental houses. From 2004 to 2006, we bought eight rental houses and three units in an apartment building in Chicago. By 2008, we realized our timing was off. If we had bought the houses a few years earlier and sold them all by 2007, we would have had a comfortable retirement. The economic downturn wiped out much of our retirement savings and, by 2010, the small business of property investment was over.

Finally, by 2012, we both had fully retired and ready to move for our final stage of life. We were tempted to think that this was stagnation, but upon reflection, it was just the opposite. It wasn't always fun, but it turned out to be productive.

Some fairly unexpected things were happening in our lives.

First, despite the fact that I was pulled in many directions all at once, I was content that I was producing things that mattered. Many of my students loved what I was offering. We were able to rescue two homeless families from shelter homes and place them in homes.

Second, my beloved wife kept charge of the books in an orderly way far better than I would ever have been able to do, and we continued to love each other through it all.

Third, the wonderful pastor and congregation at the Annunciation of the Mother of God Byzantine Catholic Church, Father Thomas J. Loya, enveloped us in their love and spiritual and intellectual stimulation sustained us through everything that happened. There was and is a spirit there that connected us with a culture that kept us connected with Christ and the Apostles.

But our business was gone. We had no stable source of income. Therefore, at age sixty-six, we both fully retired.

Chris had migraines most of her life, and despite all of our efforts nothing seemed to help. Ann Arbor, Michigan, has an internationally known headache clinic, which attracted us. Moreover, the Detroit area offers a less expensive lifestyle than does the Chicago area. Finally, there are several Byzantine Catholic Churches in the area where we could find worship. This was the autumn of 2012.

We were very sad to move away from our children and

grandchildren, but for financial and medical reasons we needed to move. Would we despair, or would we find integrity in our new and perhaps our last abode on earth?

Chapter 12

ROAD TO INTEGRITY AND CONTENTMENT

"Healthy children will not fear life if their elders have integrity enough not to fear death."

—Erik Erikson

"One daily devotion in Byzantine Christianity is to contemplate one's own mortality."

—Anonymous

"Take Pleasure in one thing and rest in it, in passing from one social act to another social act, thinking of God."

—Marcus Aurelius, *Meditations*

Despite my struggle to overcome despair, my spiritual goal was to develop ideas and people worth remembering and honoring. As I look back upon my life, I have found contentment in knowing that we helped revive some churches and encourage Christians to face life with courage and faith. I look at our sons and their children and find that they have married good women and have well-behaved and intelligent children. I appreciate their kindness toward us. I believe we have done about as well as we could in giving our sons encouragement and direction in their lives, and they seem to be passing along those directions to their children.

Yet, I wasn't fully satisfied with doing little or nothing in our full retirement. We moved to Michigan within a hundred or so miles from where I grew up, and in a suburb only a few miles from the city where Chris grew up.

One of the fulfilling tasks was to draw closer to my dying brother and his wife, who lived in the Toledo, Ohio area. We visited with them, and they came to our home to see us. We became closer than we had been since childhood. In 2010 Willie and his wife Juanita joined us in Ann Arbor prior to our move. We had a great time sharing old stories, and Wille was dressed to the nines. Imagine a blue suit, long coat, and bowler hat with a cane. He was dressed better than I had ever seen him. He was barely able to walk, but we were happy that he could dress up and show off.

Richard was the child in my mother's body when our father beat her. Richard struggled with asthma all of his life and discovered that he had diabetes later in life. He had nearly died from the latter in the mid-1990s, and after several weeks in intensive care, and after recovering enough to go back to work, he was run over by a truck in 2000. The accumulation of these problems caused him years of physical suffering. Through it all, he became a very devout Catholic man and did all he could to lead his family toward following Christ.

Richard and I spent a few days at Interlochen State Park and the Music Camp across the road in 2011. It was to be the last trip we took together. His last few weeks of life, in the spring of 2013, were spent mostly in the hospital. Our visits there were intense but with connection even though he could not speak. He would punch simple answers onto a communication board.

One request was for me to sing a simple Gospel tune, which we had learned from our grandparents.

I prayed to myself that this song and his older brother singing it to him would help him understand that his life had been rich and full and complete. He smiled throughout the song. I prayed the same for myself.

Was it one day or two that we saw him alive? I don't recall, but he took his final trip to Calvary. At his funeral, I sang it again, for him and for his family.

I don't know if Erikson was reflecting upon St. Paul's note to the Corinthian Church in I Corinthians 15 or not, but that was the effect on me. Erikson wrote, "The style of integrity developed by his culture or civilization then becomes the patrimony of his soul, the seal of his moral paternity of himself. In such final consolidation, death loses its sting."[36]

Over the years, people have frequently said to me, "You have a pastor's heart." I hope so.

My Aunt Emilee, the widow of the man on whose birthday I was born, has been a great source of strength for me. She prays for me, and for a long list of people who have been brought into her life, every day. She lives far enough away that I rarely see her, but we speak often on the phone. She has asked me to conduct her funeral. She speaks often of the joy she has just anticipating heaven and being with her husband. But most of all, she speaks of being united with her Lord Jesus Christ and seeing the Father and of rejoicing in heaven.

One day she told me of a vision, which included this phrase, which she asked that I make the theme of her funeral "Anxiously waiting for the great coronation day." Some day we shall exchange our humble robes of righteousness for a crown that will be a pronouncement that we have reached the coronation that St. Paul longed for and which is promised for those who finish the race and unite with Christ in heaven. "O what shouting. O what singing. O how we will praise Him." That will be her fulfilled patrimony. I pray that it will someday be mine as well.

Her prayers for myself and for the people I love and her longing for heaven, remind me of the yearning I felt but could not really explain even when I was seven years old and caring for the puppies who were so near death. It is the longing I had in my heart and mind and in my soul as I worked to save my mother. It is the longing that swelled up in my heart and mind as I was given the opportunity to preach my first sermon at age fifteen.

The camp meeting experience when I first openly surrendered to the yearning God gave me was accompanied by a very wonderful song.

Softly and tenderly Jesus is calling.

I hear that song more and more. I hear the tender calling in that song. I can see him waiting and watching. I can see Him calling and waiting and watching for my friends and even for my enemies.

"My enemies," yes, I have them. Most of whom have come since living in our present location. I've made many friends, but we are not only defined by our friends, but in some ways by our enemies. My few enemies only remind me of my calling to help others find their way to Christ.

I tried my hand at politics because I saw some areas where I thought I could be helpful. I ran for State Representative. Those who ran against me saw my attempt to run for office as an attack. Despite the fact that my opponent was not the incumbent, the district party had already chosen her to run well before the Primary.

I lost those elections, although I gave my opponent a good challenge. But after an appeal from many people in our town, I ran for city council. I put all of my energy into it because the more the citizens told me about the workings of the council, the more I learned about the bribery and illegal activities, the more I wished to help change things. I also saw opportunities, which the council did not wish to have anything to do with.

I recall that I was successful in helping the city of my first pastoral assignment to avoid a blue flu and to feed the homeless. I thought if I could do that, I could do this. As St. Paul wrote to the Ephesians, the world is full of "principalities and powers unseen" which cause chaos and corruption constantly. I did not win. This was not to be, so I gave up any interest in running for political office.

My good Aunt Emilee said you have more important things to do than politics. Focus on those. God has called you to pastoral ministry. She was right, of course. Through it all, my beloved remained loyal to me and my calling. She insists that I always lead in prayer. She loves me, no matter what.

She even agreed with me that we both needed strength training, and so we enrolled with Dr. Jonathon Sullivan in Greysteel Strength and Conditioning. We have both become physically stronger than at any other time in our lives.

Writing this reminds me of the work of the Good Shepherd recorded by St. John in Chapter 10. Shepherds lead their sheep and lambs into the sheepfold surrounded by stone, which the sheep will not cross with one opening for entrance and exit when the shepherd leads. At night, the shepherd lays down his life at the entrance to protect the sheep from wandering away.

It has often felt like night, and I was not sure sometimes that the shepherd was protecting the entrance. I wasn't sure that the enemies would not come in, and I wasn't even sure if I would keep from wandering off.

Being led to write this, brings a contentment I have not always felt before. The Shepherd has now come to guard this sheep. I'm thankful and content.

Chapter 13

TO THE FINAL STEP

"We're born alone, we live alone, we die alone. Only through our love and friendship can we create the illusion for the moment that we're not alone."

—Orson Welles

As I look back upon my life and try to summarize what it all has meant or perhaps what it might mean once this body is gone, I keep remembering a folk song I heard at a Nazarene Church in Adrian, Michigan. I was sixteen when I heard it, which would mean that it was in 1963. A prominent member of the church picked up his guitar and began singing a Woody Guthrie song I had never heard before, but in many circles it was very well known.

Guthrie grew up in a low-income family and wandered about the country from the 1930s into the 1960s singing songs he had written himself for the most part or had developed from earlier spirituals. I knew nothing of Woody Guthrie at that time, nor had I ever heard his "Lonesome Valley," but it keeps coming back to me as I enter the home stretch of this life.

I thought it a curious song for church. Wasn't Jesus always with us? He promised never to forsake us. Yet, didn't he have to pray alone in Gethsemane? Didn't He die alone and forsaken even by God? And aren't we commanded to pick up our own cross and follow Him?

I was not sure that this song was speaking a truth, at least not one I liked.

Nevertheless, I have known that loneliness and know it more than I know companionship, even of God. Despite the companionship of the saints I have known, despite the prayers and love of my blessed wife, loneliness seems almost to be a constant companion. It's the most profound part of the suffering that every religion knows we experience.

I've fantasized that in another life, I may enjoy monastic life or life even of the hermitage. But I enjoy the respite that comes when I'm with people, especially when I can help them. My pastoral vocation is my life.

Is there another step I need to take in the healing of the soul? Will that healing take place in this life, or will it only be in the afterlife? Is loneliness common to all humans? Is the afterlife our only true home?

As I write this, we have been in modified isolation because of the demands of government officials because of COVID-19. I suspect they know less about what is needed for the people and a good deal more about what is needed for themselves. We are in what is called a pandemic. Whenever we go outside of the house, we joke that we are escaping house arrest. It does not seem real somehow. Perhaps the experience itself is teaching us that we can be alone without being lonely.

Nevertheless, we were able to attend what we call our home church just outside of Chicago. It conducts an Orthodox liturgy in an Orthodox setting designed to bring the realm of heaven to earth. I feel at home there more than at any other place on earth. It is a break from the sense of loneliness that otherwise accompanies me.

Is this the only physical life we will lead, or as Origen wrote, God will restore all things no matter how long it takes. I tend to think his idea is somehow closer to the truth. The followers of Sanatana Dharma refer to this "restoration" as "samsara." It is a progressive emptying of "karma" from ones' soul. Catholics call this purgatory, which only the pure escape to their eventual beatific vision with God. Orthodox pray for the departed soul until it is fully healed. I like that. It seems right.

I think of these things when I dream of my parents but mostly of my father. I spent more time in my formative years with my father than with my mother, so it is not surprising that my dreams often include him.

Moreover, many of the formative years the healing of the soul included the influence of my father, even when the influences were or seemed to be quite negative. The same man who beat my pregnant mother and was a firm believer in corporal punishment was also the man who rescued Goldie's pups. There would have been no pups for me to save, if not for him. He was also the man who wrote the powerful words of encouragement on the inside cover of the Bible my parents gave me upon my graduation. His reminder to me was to never lose faith.

His aggressive behavior made me hope to be a better father and husband than he was. Maybe I have become a better "father than my father." Maybe he is on a journey to God just as I am.

My latest dream, which is really a summary of my healing soul, explains some things about my relationship with my father. In my dream, I visited him at our family home. As the house was only a driveway away from the store, I looked over to see the outside of the store, and it looked better than it had ever looked before. It still had its basic shape that it had always had, although larger. I walked over to it and entered the building. All of the inside walls had been removed, and the walls were cleaned, repaired, and prepped for brand-new things. It was much nicer, even in its barren state, than it had ever been. My father had a glow about him. He spoke with great hope for the future. He spoke of having a vision for the future.

Is this my father in the future? Will I be with him some day with God after the Lord has restored all things to Himself? I do not know, but as Archbishop Kallistos Ware said, "it is a good hope."

AFTERWORD

What has happened that helps me understand that my soul is being healed:

First, if a child expresses a sense of the presence of God and of his calling, trust that child and help them investigate and discern what the calling might be.

Second, learn to trust those you have asked for help or don't ask them for help. I could have saved myself a great deal of sorrow if I had sought guidance from those I trusted when trying to complete my dissertation.

Third, help people when they ask for it but not before. Working out one's salvation applies not only to oneself but also to others.

Fourth, following this is to understand that healing will be worked out in God's time and not ours. God's plan is a perfect restoration of all things. Origen may well be right, or at least we have some evidence to hope that the soul is not complete until it is complete, whether in this life or another. Even hell itself may not be final.

Fifth, being always precedes becoming or existence. Without Being, nothing exists, including the soul. Existence is not complete until it is enfolded back into Being. Existence is constantly changing. Teleos does not simply mean ending but completion. It may well mean restoration. The problem with some philosophies is their inability to distinguish between being and existence. Being is, while existence moves toward Being. Existence is not complete.

Sixth, I Corinthians 15 is not just as exercise in poetic metaphor. "Death is swallowed up in victory . . . The sting of death is sin, and the power of sin is law. But thanks be to God who gives us the victory through our Lord Jesus Christ" (I Corinthians 15:54 b-57). Being, i.e., God, is sovereign. His desire is to heal all things to Himself.

Seventh, as Joseph Campbell wrote, "follow your bliss and the universe will open doors where there were only walls."

Eighth, when God places a life's partner in ones' life, cherish them as you do your own body. They must never be demeaned.

Ninth, physical science is a wonderful tool for understanding the physical world, but it is only one way to understand reality. Mysticism is the purest way of knowing because it reveals the spiritual reality that underlies the physical.

I am content to await physical death and the victory of Christ that He promises. In His time.

ACKNOWLEDGMENTS

The task of writing this book was a forty-six-year task that began with an inspiration when digging in Israel and continued in 1975–76 when my dear wife sent me off to complete my initial effort on consciousness in the writings of Tertullian of Carthage. The writing has now been completed, but after many twists and turns. Many of those twists and turns were painful, but all of them were mollified by the loyalty and supported up by my precious wife, Christine Ann (McMullen) Lauffer. This project would never have been completed without her.

Acknowledgment also is given to my major professor in Garrett-Evangelical Seminary and Northwestern University, Professor Dennis Edward Groh. Acknowledgment is also given to the late Professor WHC Frend, who assisted my research in the early days of my effort when I studied at Glasgow and Oxford Universities.

Finally, I wish to acknowledge the friendship and insights given by the Reverend Thomas J. Loya, my priest at Annunciation of the Mother of God Byzantine Catholic Church, whose kindness and generosity will forever be appreciated.

We pray for the friends and enemies I've made through politics. We pray for our fellow lifters and for our coach and his wife.

We pray for the children we teach at a local Church as they move toward full confirmation and find great contentment.

We pray for and thank God for our family in their kindness, especially for Chris' sisters Lori and Val and their patient husbands who led in the rehabilitation of our condo, and to my little sister, Sherri, who has kept us in her circle of friends.

Most of all, I am thankful that God has allowed me a long enough life to write this book. For most of my life, I carried some guilt and shame for never completing my dissertation. That is to say, my conscience troubled me until the inspiration for this book came my way.

ABOUT THE AUTHOR

I was born the first of six children into a family whose parents fought until they finally divorced. At thirteen I had a conversion experience that changed the direction of my life. I preached my first sermon at age 15 at a large youth camp in Circleville, Ohio. At eighteen I boarded a bus for Illinois for college with one Robert Hall Suit, $40 saved from working all summer, and a promise of a full-time job to pay for my college.

During college I helped start a small rural congregation with the aid of other college students and met and married the love of my life, Christine.

After college, I entered Garrett Seminary and Northwestern

University to begin a MA program in a combination of Classical Graeco-Roman Studies and Early Christian studies. I eventually completed the MA degree, a Master's of Divinity, and all but dissertation for my PhD. During that period, I also participated in an archaeological expedition to Israel and studied at the University of Glasgow and Oxford University.

I pastored several Churches and taught at three different colleges.

I have been married to Christine Ann (McMullen) Lauffer for over 53 years. We have two sons and five grandchildren.

NOTES

1 Ephesians 6:12; and 6:10–17.

2 M. Scott Peck, People of the Lie (New York: Simon and Schuster, 1983).

3 Postmodernism is a denial of existence of any ultimate principle that lacks the optimism of their being a scientific, philosophical, or religious truth. Ironically its attack on any metaphysic leaves its own principle without any foundation. It is similar to solipsism, the denial of any objective reality. It is finally absurd.

4 Solipsism is extreme egocentrism. A belief that the self is the only existent thing. Merriam-Webster.

5 Occam's razor, Ordinatio. However, it was a common understanding by the fourteenth century. Phiralitus non est povenda sine necessitate Precedence is given to simplicity, if two competing theories exist about an entity, the simpler explanation is to be preferred.

6 Ibid, See Cicero, De Oratore

7 Dictionary.com Philosophy. Solipsism is the theory that only the self exists, or can be proved to exist. An extreme preoccupation with and indulgence of one's feelings, desires, etc.; egoistic self-absorption.

8 George Gilder, Life After Google (Washington D.C.: Regnery Publishing, 2018), 100–101.

An abstract strategy board game developed in China 2500 years ago. "Google's worldview is built on the philosophical certainty that algorithms, the 'if-then' logical elements of computer programming are supreme. Algorithms are made of numbers and logic. Godel proved you cannot, in principle, build a self-contained system of logic and math. There is always a system encompassing your system and a system outside your system that necessarily impinges on the basic rules of your system. We usually call this state of things the real world.

Gilder adds: Q: 'Why would a smart company like Google get it wrong?' Gilder: 'The advances in machine learning that Google trumpets and preens about are really just advances in the speed of processing.' The Google guys woke up with a Moore's Law bonanza from the chip industry and imagined that they had invented it. When their 'Go'-playing computer can play more 'Go' games in a minute than the whole human race has played throughout history, that's not a great advance in intelligence. It's the same intelligence just accelerated to terahertz speeds. Yet this creates an illusion of super-intelligence, that machine learning can somehow gain consciousness and usurp humans." Go is an abstract board game developed over 2500 years ago.

9 Ibid, p. 103

10 Jnana yoga expresses the discovery of reality by asking the question repeatedly "Who am I" as if one is peeling an onion. Layer by layer as the question is asked, finally reaches the central answer which is "I am soul."

11 The longer version is found among other places in: The Bible of the World (Viking Press, 1939), 259–260. Anatta is defined as "no soulness" or simply "no soul." The idea that there is no objective reality.

12 Merriam-Webster offers some helpful definitions of soul

1: the immaterial essence, animating principle, or actuating cause of an individual life

2a: the spiritual principle embodied in human beings, all rational and spiritual beings, or the universe

b: capitalized, Christian Science : GOD SENSE 1B

3: a person's total self

4a: an active or essential part

b: a moving spirit : LEADER

5a: the moral and emotional nature of human beings

b: the quality that arouses emotion and sentiment

c: spiritual or moral force : FERVOR

13 E.g., "But to be strong enough both to bear the one and to be sober in the other is the mark of a man, a perfect and invincible soul, such as he showed . . ."

14 Ephesian 1:4 "...just as he chose us in Christ before the foundation of the world to be holy and blameless before him in love."

Jeremiah 1:5 "Before I formed you in the womb I knew you,

and before you were born I consecrated you;

I appointed you a prophet to the nations."

15 Erik Erikson, Childhood and Society (New York: W.W. Norton, 1985), 251.

16 Ibid, p. 252.

17 Ibid, p. 253.

18 Childhood and Society, p. 257.

19 A beautiful illustration of this is found in the separation between the holy of holies in the ancient Jewish temple and the common area. The same is true in many churches that have an altar, which is sometimes called a mourners' bench. It is most dramatically seen in the architecture of Orthodox and Eastern Catholic Churches in the Iconostasis. All of these separations are also an invitation from the saints to move away from indolence and strife and toward holiness residing in heaven. All are profound ways to connect consciousness residing In the soul with the Divine Consciousness which is God.

20 Childhood and Society, pp. 258–261.

21 Childhood and Society, p. 262.

22 Childhood and Society, p. 263.

23 Childhood and Society, p. 266.

24 St. Irenaeus, Adversus Haereses, IV.38; St. Athanasius, Against Arius, I.39; III.34; On the Incarnation, 54.

25 Justin Martyr, Apologia I.5-6

26 "The Depiction of Ancient Greek Philosophers in Orthodox Churches", omhksea.org

27 Tatian, Address to the Greeks, VI.1; Irenaeus, Against Heresies, V.3,2;V.12,1; IV.38.1; Clement of Alexandria, Stromata, VI.6,52,1.

28 Origen, First Principles.

29 Daniel B. Clendenin, Eastern Orthodox Christianity: A Western Perspective (Grand Rapids: Baker, 1994).

30 Gerald L. Bray, "Deification," in Sinclair InterVarsity, 1988).

31 Rowan Williams, "Deification," in Gordon S. Wakefield, ed., The Westminster Dictionary of Christian Spirituality (Philadelphia: Westminster, 1983).

Philip Edgecumbe Hughes, The True Image (Grand Rapids: Eerdmans, 1989).

Various scriptures used include: I Peter 1:8b–9 "You rejoice with an indescribable joy, as you attain the goal of faith, the salvation of your souls." The soul becomes healed or saved when it reaches unity with God. 2 Peter 1:3–4 "His divine power has granted to us all things that pertain to life and godliness, through the knowledge of him who called us to his own glory and excellence, by which he has granted to us his precious and very great promises, that through these you may escape from the corruption that is in the world because of passion, and become partakers of the divine nature.

32 Childhood and Society, p. 267.

33 Andre Dolbecq and Andrew VandeVen, Journal of Applied Behavioral Science, (1971) 7, 466–91 and Dolbecq and VandeVen, "Group Techniques for Program Planning", (1975), Glenview, IL, Scott-Foresman and Co.

34 The Book of Discipline of the United Methodist Church, 1984, paragraph 402.2.

35 Childhood and Society, p. 268.

36 Childhood and Society, p. 269.

Made in United States
North Haven, CT
19 October 2021

10436716R00076